Romance of
AUSTRALIAN
RAILWAYS

PATSY ADAM SMITH'S
romance of
AUSTRALIAN RAILWAYS

LONDON:
ROBERT HALE & COMPANY

ADELAIDE:
RIGBY LIMITED

First published in Great Britain 1974
Copyright © 1974 Patsy Adam Smith

ISBN 0 7091 4204 8

Robert Hale & Company
63 Old Brompton Road
London SW7 3JU

Printed in Hong Kong

CONTENTS

ACKNOWLEDGMENTS

The help for a book such as this comes from a wide canvas—ranging from signalmen who invited me up to the box "to see how it really works" to librarians who helped me in my search for manuscript material.

My grateful thanks are especially due to the La Trobe Library staff of the State Library of Victoria, for making available such a wealth of material from their vast railways collection. Thanks are also due to the staffs of the Mitchell Library, Sydney; the Battye Library, Perth; the Oxley Library, Brisbane; the State Archives, State Library of South Australia, Adelaide; and the State Library of Tasmania.

The railways systems of the various States and the Commonwealth have published a considerable amount of material in pamphlets and information sheets, and these have been used without acknowledgment in the text. Excerpts from newspapers and periodicals, and unpublished manuscripts, are acknowledged in the text and listed in the bibliography.

Grateful acknowledgment is made to the following for permission to reproduce published material: The Estate of Mrs Gunn and the Hutchinson Publishing Group, Ltd, for an extract from *We of the Never Never* by Mrs Aeneas Gunn; Angus & Robertson (Publishers) Pty Ltd, for the poem "The Flying Gang" by A. B. Paterson, from the book *The Collected Verse of A. B. Paterson*; John Murray (Publishers) Ltd, for an extract from *The Dead Heart of Australia* by J. W. Gregory.

My thanks for photographic material are due to the various State Libraries and Archives mentioned above, and also the following: Winter's Studios, Burnie, Tasmania, for many of the West Coast of Tasmania photographs; Australia and New Zealand Railways Conferences, for their excellent liaison work with the various State and Commonwealth railway systems; Mr Ron Grant of the South Australian Railways Institute; and Mr Douglas Luck, who provided a large portion of the colour transparencies.

As well, there are the many railway workers who have given me unpublished material. I hope this record of their work will in some small way be a memorial to their labours in an age that has truly ended.

An 1877 sketch of Flinders Street Railway Station. Advertisers clamour for the passenger's attention in what was said to be a more "leisurely" age

WHEN WE RODE THE RAILS

THE MELBOURNE *Argus* on 12 September 1854 said, "The shrill tones of the steam whistle will indicate today, as significantly as if the cannon were booming in celebration of our independence, that a new era has dawned upon us." From that day, when the first "shrill tones" shrieked out over the nation and the first train fled across the land, we Australians seemed to ride the rails and travel the tracks as though to the manner born. Farmers, politicians, polite society, and Bradshaw's themselves slid into the railway age as if we'd known no other, and, in a way, we had not. England had known a time dating back to mythology when she knew no steam engine; but we did not. By the time the First Fleet arrived in Botany Bay with new settlers willing and unwilling, James Watt had developed the steam engine in their homeland. By 1801, Richard Trevithick had run a locomotive on rails. Few Australian settlements were founded before the time that George Stephenson's Locomotive No. 1 ran on the Stockton and Darlington Railway in 1825, so along with the enthusiasm to set up a new nation we brought with us the knowledge of railways. Some, like the Melbourne *Argus,* were pompous about it. "That grand career of material progress,

Editor to Sub-Editor: "What! No murders or accidents? Oh, well, have another go at the Railways!—Yes—about a column; Make it pretty hot; couldn't get a seat coming in this morning!"

Above: *Railway folk at Oodnadatta, South Australia, on the central Australian line, in 1908*

Below: *Woodend (Victoria) Station and staff, October 1870. The American influence on Australian railways is obvious from the smoke stacks on the two locomotives*

A Western Australian A class narrow gauge locomotive hauling "dog box" carriages

which has become the distinguishing characteristic of modern civilization," it pontificated. An anonymous politician (whose identity was known to everyone) campaigned on a platform of RAILWAYS AND PROGRESS, with a six paged magazine titled *Railwayiana* in which he referred to himself as The Wizard. The illustrations depicted him on the footplate of a locomotive, with his hand on the throttle of destiny.

It was as though nothing would ever be the same again once railways got under way—and for a hundred years much of the country agreed with this. For in that period, The Railway Age as some men called it, there was little of our living, our workaday or social life not affected by the lonesome whistle that winkled its way into every corner of the land. Thoroughfares given the proud names of Railway Road and Station Street became the hubs of the larger towns, while the stations themselves became the centres of widespread country areas; equivalents of the parish-pumps, where news was spread and isolation eased for a time while we "waited for the train to come in." We didn't necessarily wait for anyone or anything on the train. It was the waiting that counted, and the train itself when it came. It brought a whiff of other places, other people; the daily—or weekly—reminder that we lonely ones were not alone, that there were plenty of others like us in this big country, probably battling like us to settle, to get this untamed and unbroken place by the throat. There were the wheat trains, the spud trains, the wool trains, the Show Trains, and the excursions. Wherever we lived there was a train for what we produced or for where we wanted to go and a train to remind us of the greener pastures in other places.

When we rode the rails the land was rosy and young, and so were we.

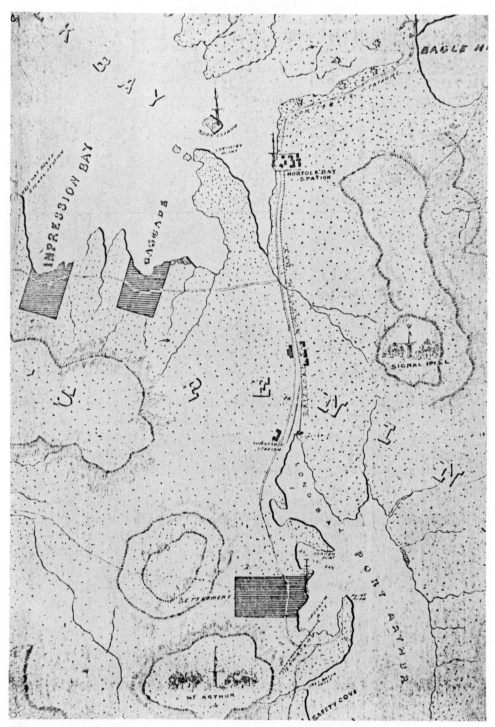

The route of the 1836 convict-powered railway, linking what is now Taranna and Oakwood, Tasmania

HALLOOING, SHOUTING, SCREAMING LIKE MADMEN

WHEN THE RAILWAYS, the *real railways,* came, no one wanted to remember the other sort; the horse-drawn railways, or the one-and-only railway propelled by manpower. Some refused even to dignify them by such a name and insisted on calling them Tramways, even when giant locomotives running on standard gauge iron rails had become known in some places as Tramways.

The definition of a railway as "a conveyance for passengers and freight, drawn along fixed parallel rails by motive power under statutory authority," fits the 1836 convict railway at Port Arthur, Van Diemen's Land—except for the motive power. This earliest of "trains" in Australia fitted the other qualifications, and performed a painfully necessary service: that of enabling passengers to avoid the sea trip around Cape Raoul, which seamen to this day describe as "Rounding the Raoul means having the guts rolled out of you."

Australia's first railway line ran for about four and a half miles, from what is today the little centre of Taranna, across Tasman Peninsula, to Oakwood. It was built twenty years before steam trains came to Australia with the opening of the Melbourne

A contemporary lithograph of the convict railway, Tasmania. Note the convicts riding downhill on the carriage to the right

Above: *Horse-drawn trains remained until the twentieth century, as this 1907 photograph shows on the Port Broughton to Mundoora line, South Australia.*

Facing Page: *A full load on the Dunkley town tram, Tasmania*

line in 1854. Before that, the power that Tasmania had most of was manpower, so their first train was propelled by convicts. The use of men to push trucks carrying other men was to incense and disgust people all through the years after the little line stopped work.

The railway was the brain child of Captain O'Hara Booth, the Commandant of the convict settlement at Port Arthur. He planned the line to save passengers from Hobart the rough sea voyage across Storm Bay and around Tasman Island to Port Arthur. Ships from Hobart would anchor in Norfolk Bay and boat their passengers ashore, who would climb up on the carriages that looked like hay carts and set off under convict-power to Long Bay. From here, Port Arthur is only three miles by sea or land.

In 1836, O'Hara put convicts to work constructing the earthworks. They were the first men in Australia to be employed as "navvies"—a term that originated in England when labourers who dug the network of barge canals across Britain, before and after the railways came, were jokingly called "navigators." This was soon shortened to "navvy," and was applied to men building earthworks and embankments for the railways instead of digging canals.

According to an early commuter, the convict line was no great engineering feat. He said, "The tramway, unlike our English railways, follows the natural levels of the ground, the ascent of the hill being compensated in its opposite descent." The rails were of wood fashioned from gum trees cut beside the track. They were about six inches wide and were fastened onto sleepers spaced a foot apart. According to Lady Franklin, wife of Sir John, the Governor, the timber was laid down green. She wrote in her journal, on 22 March 1837, that when she saw the railway Captain Booth told her it was not looking as good as usual. He said, "The road is suffered to be clogged with sand at present that the sun may have less power on it." Her story goes to prove one thing; that railway men from the beginning were never short of a quick answer.

Contrary to what most writers have suggested, Lady Franklin did not see the railway at work nor travel on it. Instead, she was carried down the track on a kind of sedan chair, made in true Bunyip Aristocracy style of kangaroo skins spread over boards attached to two poles. These, she said, were "strapped to two yellow men." This suggests Asian coolies, but she referred to the convicts who wore sulphur-coloured uniforms marked with the broad arrow.

Lady Franklin believed that three convicts drew the "carts," as she called them; one harnessed in front to pull, while two pushed from behind. Her statement is the foundation on which most writers base their comparison of the convicts to beasts of burden. The fact is that, if they were ever harnessed in front, it must have been only in the very early stage. They would soon find, as men have done throughout history, that the human body can push better than it can pull. It is not likely that the convict overseers would fail to get the best out of the men in their charge, so they would certainly all be pushers, not pullers. And just as well, because Lady Franklin goes on to say that the track followed the contours of the land. "Gentle rises and falls are preserved," she wrote. "Propelling the carts down raises them up again to the other side." Lady Jane did not mention how the man whom she presumed to be harnessed in front was going to skip out of the way when the train came rattling down the slopes hard on his heels.

A better description was given by Captain Stonor, who wrote the book *A Year in Tasmania*. He said, "The rail carriages if they can be called that are of a very rude construction, very low, double seated, with four very small cast iron wheels. On either side project two long handles which the prisoners lean on to propel the carriage. The road being not exactly level but containing many ascents and descents forms a very amusing transit to a stranger, for as you rise the incline the prisoners puff and blow pushing on

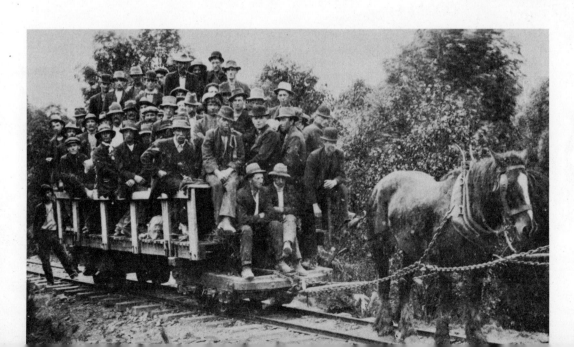

Above and below: *South Australia's claim to the first Australian railway was this five foot three inch gauge horse line, between Goolwa and Port Elliot. The seven-mile line was installed to provide a connecting link between the Murray River steamers and sea-going ships*

The original No. 1 locomotive of the Victorian Railways Department—the first passenger engine on the Melbourne and Hobson's Bay Company line (1854)

The first orthodox locomotive built in Australia, and placed in service on the Melbourne to Hobson's Bay Company line

Left: *Locomotive No. 1210 hauled the first train to the site of Canberra in 1914*

Immediately below: *An American-built ten-wheeler Baldwin locomotive, from the Iron Knob-Whyalla line, South Australia*

Bottom of page: *An R class locomotive placed in service in 1899 in Western Australia, involved in the Bonnievale mine special of 1907*

Above: *The Sandfly is believed to have spent its working life shunting at Darwin, then known as Palmerston. It is now preserved at Port Augusta*

Faithful haulers of desert trains, G class steam locomotives were in use on the Trans-Australian Railway from 1917-52.

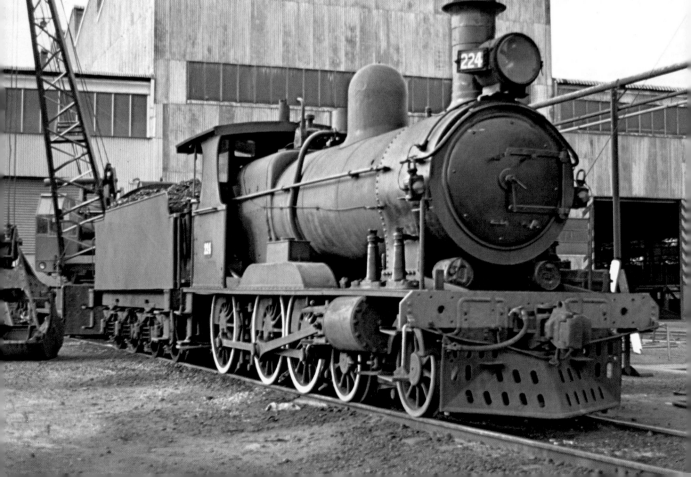

Facing page, top: *Tandem Rx class locomotives (South Australian Railways) near Riverton. Eighty-four of this class (also* facing page, bottom*) were still in service on 30 June 1967 when broad-gauge steam working ceased in South Australia.*
Above: *An F class "Dolly" tank engine introduced in South Australia from 1902-22. All forty-three engines in service were built in the State and were used on suburban passenger trains until replaced by diesel rail cars from 1956-67.*

Above: *The Y class locomotives were the most abundant on the South Australian Railways (137) and Silverton Tramway Company (New South Wales) 3' 6" lines. Similar engines served with the Commonwealth Railways, Western Australian Government Railways, Tasmanian Government Railways, and on many private timber and ore lines.*

Below: *This Silverton Tramway Company A class locomotive introduced in 1915 served on the thirty-three miles of Company line from Broken Hill to the South Australian border.*

the carriage but when descending up they jump alongside of you and away you go, dashing, crashing, tearing on. Half-way along the line is a half-way rest station (here the crew is changed), as you have a considerable ascent for nearly a mile and then a like descent to the jetty which is quite a nervous affair, and as the speed increases each moment you expect to be dashed over into some precipice or deep jungle alongside the tram. An upset sometimes does happen but is seldom serious. There is always a director with the train who can check the wheels with a drag."

Several passengers have left records of the rest house at the half-way mark. It was a substantial log hut where the fettling gang of twenty men were quartered. There was another hut at each end of the track. Frederick Mackie, a Quaker missionary, rode on the railway in 1853 and describes in his journal the distress he felt at seeing men used for such labour. He was, however, permitted to give them "a small reward;" in other words, a tip. According to Mackie, four men propelled the train. Lieutenant-Colonel Godfrey Mundy's book *Our Antipodes* shows this type of wagon with four men pushing *up*-hill while in a separate cart or carriage four men sit with their feet up resting as they career *down*-hill. The sketch, executed in lithography by W. L. Walton, has been reproduced probably more times than any other railway picture in Australian history. It shows the "permanent way" crossing a stream in a heavily forested area. Today a walker along the old track can almost pinpoint the spot, about a mile from the southern end of the line near the head of the inlet.

The route of the earthworks can be picked up at spots along from the old stone jetty, which is partly covered by a collapsed "newer" timber jetty, half a mile from the northern end of Long Bay. You can find odd bits of timber that may or may not have been used in culverts. It doesn't matter; the search is the thing. The whole line crossed country lovely in springtime, thick with pink, red, and cream heath and stunted little golden wattles. And blackberries. Off Joyners Link Road on the way to Port Arthur the earthworks of the old track show up clearly when the grass dries off in autumn. The structures have all gone, including the solid wooden huts at either end and in the middle of the line. Probably our best record of what the railway looked like is in old stills from the 1910 movie *The Term of His Natural Life* when the railway was reconstructed— fairly accurately—for the heroine to ride, while poor Dawes, the ill-fated convict, pushed the truck for her and her wicked husband. A map known to have been in existence in 1877 shows the railway as having a branch line to a Constable's Station beside the road to Port Arthur. This would make it possible to complete the journey by land rather than by sea.

Many travellers wrote about this man-traction railway. In the *Tasmanian Journal of Natural Sciences,* David Burn wrote a very lofty survey as he saw it in 1842. He reminds his reader that the railway is the brain child of Captain Booth, Commandant at Port Arthur. "Like many men of superior intellect he faced the sneers of the common herd, who, in their narrow-mindedness, predicted naught but failure in his enterprise." But ". . . nothing daunted, Captain Booth toiled on until they who came to jeer went back to admire." Burn tells of the convict workmen, who, "upon emergency have made their three journeys and back, thirty miles a day, conveying thus half-a-ton per man either way.

"It jars harshly against the feeling to behold man as it were lowered to the standard of the brute, to mark the unhappy guilty creatures toiling and struggling along, their muscular powers exerted to the utmost and the perspiration bursting from every pore. It is a harrowing picture and yet a little calm reflection will show that it is rendered more peculiarly so by place and circumstance. Let us remember that there are hundreds of free British labourers whose drudgery is fully equal to that on this tramway."

On his return journey Burn wrote "we had no idea of the speed of the tramway. There is a shoot of a mile and a half near the head of Long Bay which is traversed at the rate of forty miles an hour. It requires some little nerve at first to keep one's composure, because, once in motion, there are no stoppages, and the least obstruction would, as Jonathan says, 'Send carriages and their contents to immortal smash.'

"The officers of the French frigate *Artemise* were in ecstasies with their descent, which, on a larger scale, reminded them of the Montagnes Russes of Paris: down they went, hallooing, shouting, screaming like madmen."

The next claimant to being an earlier railway than Melbourne's was the Goolwa horse-drawn tram in South Australia. This was a proper little railway with a most ambitious intention. With its horse-powered tram and seven miles of track, South Australia intended to drain off the wealth of western New South Wales and Queensland. The colony which had less arable land than any of the others was going to ride on the sheep's back. South Australians would poach over the borders, and bring down the wool on paddle-steamers skippered by men who swore they could steam their shallow-bottomed craft "over a light dew . . . even, at a pinch, across a damped-down flour sack." These men would bring wool down the Darling, Murrumbidgee, and Lachlan into the Murray, the greatest of them all, then down that most noble river to where it joined the sea. There, at Goolwa, the freight would be transferred to the train, and hauled by "animal traction" to Port Elliot, a little under seven miles away.

There was plenty of opposition to the animal traction—we do not seem to have had a railway that got under way without opposition, even that hauled by other men.

But Sir Henry Fox Young, Governor of South Australia, approved of the little line at Goolwa. He went up the Murray with Captain Cadell, the Grand Old Man who was one of the first two riverboat men, and saw that if a connection could be made between the Murray and a seaport then, "the whole of the traffic of the interior would be diverted to South Australia." He could see his State attracting all the produce of stations carting wool to the Lachlan, Murrumbidgee, Lower Darling and Murray.

Soon the work got under way, and the colonists were so anxious to employ the line that they used the finished sections from as early as December 1853, bridging the gap by bullock dray. To them, the railway was such a practical operation that when the single horse trotted along the completed permanent way on 18 May 1854, hauling the "train," they didn't bother with an official opening—and so missed out on the great spread that signalled the opening of every railway in the land from then on. Unfortunately, the great scheme was aborted because Port Elliot is too small and exposed to be a viable seaport. It was not until the permanent way was laid from Milang to Port Adelaide that the transport gap could be closed—and by that time the paddle-steamers were being successfully challenged by the railways.

An example of a Tasmanian horse-drawn timber line, loaded with a giant log over six feet in diameter.

The greatest concentration of "animal traction lines" was on the West Coast of Tasmania; "the wild and woolly West Coast" as it was known from the beginning.

So vast and impenetrable was its location that a road was not driven through from the eastern, populous part of the State until 1936, and it is said this would not have been achieved but for the hungry years of the Depression, when men on the dole, too desperate to refuse, were put to work to build it. A road outlet to the north of the island was not completed until the mid-1960s. It had to be carved through the ravines, precipitous mountains, and, worst of all hazards in that area, the scrub of bauera and horizontal. Horizontal, a scrubby tree-like shrub, grows up to ten feet high, falls over horizontally, and sends up new shoots. These repeat the process over and over again, until it is impossible to walk under or through it. At risk of a broken limb— or worse— men have crawled over it, though a journalist who was thought to have done this in the 1940s has not been seen since. Bauera is a wiry, tough, man-defying rambling-rose type of plant, that has restricted the progress of exploring parties to as little as half a mile in eight hours.

After the first mining rush in 1850, there were 130 people, including four women, in Zeehan. These increased to 4,500 when silver-lead was discovered in 1890, and by 1899 the population was over 10,000.

The 800 square miles of the West Coast of Tasmania, with Zeehan as its centre, are enormously rich in minerals. Gold, silver, copper, tin, lead, zinc, iron, coal, sulphur, nickel, bismuth, tungsten, molybdenite, platinum, osmiridium, palladium, iridium, antimony, and barium have all been discovered there. There was a gold rush in 1879, when men from as far afield as California staked claims.

Deep gorges and mountains, that even today prohibit closer settlement of the area,

Above: *The Tullah, Tasmania, horse-drawn tram, 1907. The Spartan accommodation must have added to the thrill of the ride.*

Below: *The Emu Bay Railway, Tasmania. The horse-drawn trains were hauled over wooden rails laid on sleepers of myrtle and stringybark. The forty-five mile track carried passengers as well as tin from Mount Bischoff*

prevented entry from the eastern side of the island. The only entry to the West Coast was by sea, along the coast that is still regarded by seamen as the most treacherous and least sheltered of all Australian waters.

In 1872 Philosopher Smith, the old Tasmanian bushman, brought in samples from Mount Bischoff. From that day onwards, the mountain was known only as "the Mountain of Tin," until it was eaten up and disappeared forever. It was the richest tin mine in the world. Down in Hobart and across in Launceston the city folk were still arguing about railways, but while they held their interminable noisy meetings the Van Diemen's Land Company put down a line from Emu Bay (now known as Burnie) and horse-drawn trucks set off to haul out the riches. The track, forty-five miles long, was the longest horse-powered tramway in the British Empire, with a regular passenger and freight service. The local agent of the company was Edward Curr, whose grandfather, John Curr, was a pioneer of iron railway lines. This was a radical enterprise, described in Edward Curr's memoirs.

John Curr, brought up as a civil engineer, became steward to the Duke of Norfolk when about twenty-one, and lived in Sheffield for many years until he died in 1823. He managed the estates and coal mines of the Duke of Norfolk at a time when coal was brought from the mouth of the pit in vehicles which ran on wooden rails, and John Curr realised that a great saving would come from the use of iron rails, which up to then were unknown.

He wrote to his father, a rugged old "coal mine viewer" in Northumberland, telling him that he had decided to substitute iron rails for the wooden rails. The old man replied in a curt letter ending, "If you put down the iron rails, Jack, I curse you; and here is my hand on it!" with an outline of his "stalwart hand" traced on the back of the page. This denunciation made John Curr abandon the project, until he dined with a priest and mentioned it to him. The priest said that his duty was to his employer, so Curr had iron rails made and laid. The conservative colliers were so furious that they "threatened to take his life, so that he hid himself in a wood for three days, until the ferment had somewhat subsided."

The Van Diemen's Land Company was London-based, and formed to take up land "beyond the ramparts of the unknown." But even despite the great bite which they took out of the north-west, they still missed the mountain of tin by two miles. Their track terminated at Rowses Farm, two miles from the Mountain of Tin, and the horses turned around and headed back for Emu Bay at that point because the company could not obtain a right of way through the farm. The passengers, and the men who carried the freight on their shoulders for the rest of the way, had to plod through two miles of mud constantly replenished by the second highest rainfall in Australia.

Navvies imported from Victoria built the three foot gauge of wooden rails, laid on sleepers of myrtle and stringybark. All material was found on Company land, including the ballast quarried nearby. The local timber expanded in winter and shrank in summer and made for an interesting journey. The navvies were quartered in tents in the wet jungle beside the track where snowfalls of four feet a night are recorded and drifts of nine feet occur most winters. With pick and shovel only, they cut through the mountains that swept up to 2,023 feet at Guildford Junction, the highest station in

Tasmania, and through land that few men had trod. Those that had done so spoke shudderingly of "fearful gulphs" and "frightful chasms." The navvies laid down curves no more acute than five chains, and gradients that were never steeper than 1 in 34. When the line was built over the full eighty-eight miles to Zeehan in later years, 726 bends helped it round the "gulphs" and "chasms." All this they did for ninepence an hour, working for ten hours a day.

The little train trotted off on its "down" trip on Mondays, Wednesdays, and Fridays, and trotted back "up" on Tuesdays, Thursdays, and Saturdays. So great was the patronage that often freight and passengers were refused because of volume of traffic.

The horses did the trip in seven or eight hours, except when snow blocked the line or one of them played up, and then it could take anything up to fourteen hours. They were changed, stabled, and rested every ten miles and they needed it: during the first thirty miles out of Burnie, they climbed 2,000 feet.

The crumbling remains of their stables and the ruins of the old boarding house at Bulgobac are now the only monument to the horses and the men who built the line that later became the Emu Bay Railway, one of the few private railways to survive in Australia until our time. The jungle-like growth has covered all signs of Que, that the old-timers swear was named for the queue that formed outside the brothel set up for the 600 navvies working there; and only the painted sign remains at Boko, named for a railwayman with a big, bulbous nose.

In those days, horses were bred in Australia with such enthusiasm that it's a wonder our granddads admitted to steam having any advantage. The "hay-burners" hauled timber trains, ore trains, and produce trains. As late as 1902, by which time each State had steam trains, a horse-drawn tramway was laid down in western Tasmania as the first outlet from Tullah, a mountain fastness that had no road until 1963. A resident of Tullah, Mrs E. Richardson, remembered travelling on it. She said, "It had wooden rails and horses pulled. Good strong horses. One day when I was a girl I was coming home to Tullah and a bird flew in front of the lead horse. The horse shied and bolted, and our carriage was turned over, rolled on its side. No, nobody was hurt, except the Singer sewing-machine lady. We hit heads. I was all right. She had a lump. But she hung on to her sewing machine on her knee. She used to come in once a year to sell and repair machines in Tullah. That would be about 1908. I remember the driver. It was Bernie Daly. He drove the four horses; you needed four because of the mountains. Bernie had a pocketful of pebbles and he had a shanghai and to make a horse hurry up he'd shanghai a pebble at it and flip it on the ear. He was very good at this."

For over half a century, Australians bred horses to haul trucks along the permanent way. Not the draught, nor even the half-draught, but a coach horse was the most suitable; a horse that could make speed. After all, the coach was on rails, not a rough road, and the track was to some degree levelled. A horse that needed great amounts of food—such as the giant Clydesdales—would be useless in an area like Tasmania's feed-less West Coast, where every ounce of food must be carted in from outside. The railway needed horses with good fetlocks, strong ankles; horses much like the walers bred as Indian Army remounts for fifty years. They were less likely to go lame than a heavier horse, able to sustain power for a considerable period over rough terrain, and to supply smart bursts of speed. These horses provided a good weight-power combination.

In Australia, the occasional opposition to any sort of railway at all was peculiar and parochial, but the first Williamstown-Melbourne railway aroused some complex objections. The *Argus* reported on 8 September 1851 that at a meeting convened by the Mayor of Melbourne in the Mechanics Institute to consider construction of a railway from Melbourne "to the beach" (Williamstown), a Mr Amman spoke of his plans. He had thought of a scheme to cut away the bar at the river mouth and dig a canal for the one and a half miles to Melbourne. Instead, he favoured a railway, because if a canal were dug to connect the seaport with the town "the sailors would be amongst the townspeople." He considered that "they would be quite close enough at a distance of a mile and a half." A shipmaster, Captain Harrison, rose to the defence of his shipmates. "As far as Melbourne being contaminated by the close proximity of sailors" was concerned, he, "as a nautical man," would admit that "sailors were very dangerous characters and moreover they had generally proved so. It was true that contamination was to be dreaded, but it was from convicts not from sailors." After this ambiguity he went on to say he knew nothing about railways but did know about "mud-ways." The other day the gig he travelled in, which could be lifted by a strong man, was bogged "in the main artery of communication—the road to Sydney." This took place ten miles from Melbourne and he had to lift the vehicle out of the mire by levers.

The opposition to a railway ran in favour of a canal. "However desirable a railway might be," said a Mr Kentish, "it would be utter ruin to attempt it, for the express reason that it would be the manner to defeat the design of nature: to make Melbourne one of the finest sea-port towns in the known world."

Mr Kentish told the meeting that he was a canal man of thirty years standing. It was "the opinion of every man of sense," he said, adding "as well as myself," that however great the expense might be of making a canal, the cost would be recouped from sales of land on the canal banks.

The Yarra came in for a deal of reproof. A suggestion that warehouses could be built on its banks got the reply that it was fit for nothing else. "The locality is so unhealthy that no one would live there if he could help it." Another speaker said that, "It has lately become fashionable to abuse our friend the Yarra; some had said that our old friend was not, any longer, able to supply us with water, and now it would be said that it could not bring our ships."

Melbourne was unhappy. Its rival, "the commerce capital" Geelong, had a fine harbour, and no matter how they spoke of the Yarra being "designed by nature as a highway to Melbourne," of the removal of the bar giving "as large a bay as that of Venice" and of making Melbourne "a great maritime city," they were afraid that if they had to rely on railways to bring their goods the mile and a half from the port then it was "an acknowledgement of Geelong supremacy." It was said that, "If the vessels are always at Hobson's Bay, Melbourne will never become a place of any great magnitude."

Those in favour of a canal in preference to a railway slyly pointed out that it would take considerable time to get rails for a line out from England but, "a canal could be commenced instantly as there were so many diggers out of work."

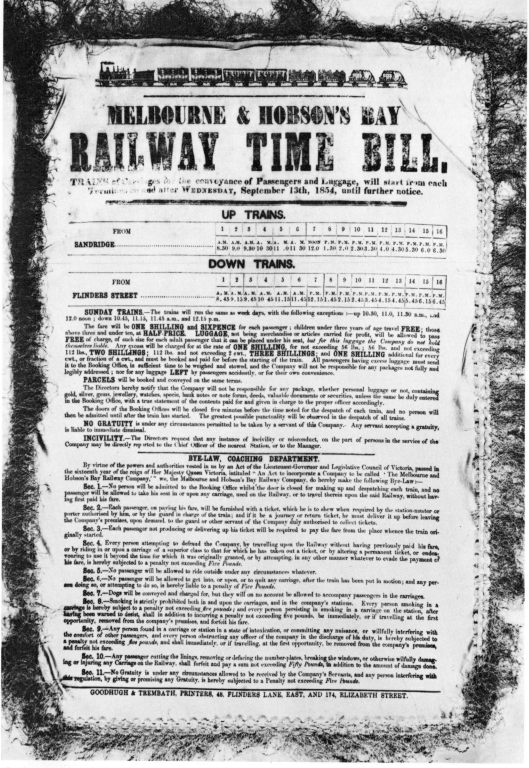

MELBOURNE & HOBSON'S BAY
RAILWAY TIME BILL.

TRAINS of Carriages for the conveyance of Passengers and Luggage, will start from each Terminus on and after WEDNESDAY, September 13th, 1854, until further notice.

UP TRAINS.

FROM	1	2	3	4	5	6	7	8	9	10	11	12	13	14	15	16
	A.M.	A.M.	A.M	M.A.	M.A.	M.A.	NOON	P.M.	P.M.	P.M	P.M	P.M	P.M	P.M	P.M.	P.M.
SANDRIDGE	8.30	9.0	9.30	10 .30	11 .0	11 .30	12.0	1.30	2.0	2.30	3.30	4.0	4.30	5.30	6.0	6.30

DOWN TRAINS.

FROM	1	2	3	4	5	6	7	8	9	10	11	12	13	14	15	16
	A.M.	A.M.	A.M.	A.M.	A.M.	A.M.	P.M.	P.M.	P.M.	P.M	P.M	P.M	P.M	P.M	P.M.	P.M.
FLINDERS STREET	8. 45	9.15	9.45	10 .45	11.15	11. 45	12.15	1.45	2.15	2.45	3.45	4.15	4.45	5.45	6.15	6.45

SUNDAY TRAINS.—The trains will run the same as week days, with the following exceptions :—up 10.30, 11.0, 11.30 a.m., and 12.0 noon ; down 10.45, 11.15, 11.45 a.m., and 12.15 p.m.

The fare will be **ONE SHILLING and SIXPENCE** for each passenger ; children under three years of age travel **FREE**; those above three and under ten, at **HALF-PRICE**. **LUGGAGE**, not being merchandise or articles carried for profit, will be allowed to pass **FREE** of charge, of such size for each adult passenger that it can be placed under his seat, *but for this luggage the Company do not hold themselves liable*. Any excess will be charged for at the rate of **ONE SHILLING**, for not exceeding 56 lbs. ; 56 lbs. and not exceeding 112 lbs., **TWO SHILLINGS**; 112 lbs. and not exceeding 2 cwt. **THREE SHILLINGS**; and **ONE SHILLING** additional for every cwt., or fraction of a cwt., and must be booked and paid for before the starting of the train. All passengers having excess luggage must send it to the Booking Office, in sufficient time to be weighed and stowed, and the Company will not be responsible for any packages not fully and legibly addressed ; nor for any luggage **LEFT** by passengers accidently, or for their own convenience.

PARCELS will be booked and conveyed on the same terms.

The Directors hereby notify that the Company will not be responsible for any package, whether personal luggage or not, containing gold, silver, gems, jewellery, watches, specie, bank notes or note forms, deeds, valuable documents or securities, unless the same be duly entered in the Booking Office, with a true statement of the contents paid for and given in charge to the proper officer accordingly.

The doors of the Booking Offices will be closed five minutes before the time noted for the despatch of each train, and no person will then be admitted until after the train has started. The greatest possible punctuality will be observed in the despatch of all trains.

NO GRATUITY is under any circumstances permitted to be taken by a servant of this Company. Any servant accepting a gratuity, is liable to immediate dismissal.

INCIVILITY.—The Directors request that any instance of incivility or misconduct, on the part of persons in the service of the Company may be directly reported to the Chief Officer of the nearest Station, or to the Manager.

BYE-LAW, COACHING DEPARTMENT.

By virtue of the powers and authorities vested in us by an Act of the Lieutenant-Governor and Legislative Council of Victoria, passed in the sixteenth year of the reign of Her Majesty Queen Victoria, intituled "An Act to incorporate a Company to be called ' The Melbourne and Hobson's Bay Railway Company,' " we, the Melbourne and Hobson's Bay Railway Company, do hereby make the following Bye-Law :—

Sec. 1.—No person will be admitted to the Booking Office whilst the door is closed for making up and despatching each train, and no passenger will be allowed to take his seat in or upon any carriage, used on the Railway, or to travel therein upon the said Railway, without having first paid his fare.

Sec. 2.—Each passenger, on paying his fare, will be furnished with a ticket, which he is to shew when required by the station-master or porter authorised by him, or by the guard in charge of the train; and if it be a journey or return ticket, he must deliver it up before leaving the Company's premises, upon demand, to the guard or other servant of the Company duly authorised to collect tickets.

Sec. 3.—Each passenger not producing or delivering up his ticket will be required to pay the fare from the place whence the train originally started.

Sec. 4.—Every person attempting to defraud the Company, by travelling upon the Railway without having previously paid his fare, or by riding in or upon a carriage of a superior class to that for which he has taken out a ticket, or by altering a permanent ticket, or endeavouring to use it beyond the time for which it was originally granted, or by attempting, in any other manner whatever to evade the payment of his fare, is hereby subjected to a penalty not exceeding *Five Pounds*.

Sec. 5.—No passenger will be allowed to ride outside under any circumstances whatever.

Sec. 6.—No passenger will be allowed to get into, or upon, or to quit any carriage, after the train has been put in motion; and any person doing so, or attempting to do so, is hereby liable to a penalty of *Five Pounds*.

Sec. 7.—Dogs will be conveyed and charged for, but they will on no account be allowed to accompany passengers in the carriages.

Sec. 8.—Smoking is strictly prohibited both in and upon the carriages, and in the company's stations. Every person smoking in a carriage is hereby subject to a penalty not exceeding *five pounds* ; and every person persisting in smoking in a carriage on the station, after having been warned to desist, shall in addition to incurring a penalty not exceeding five pounds, be immediately, or if travelling at the first opportunity, removed from the company's premises, and forfeit his fare.

Sec. 9.—Any person found in a carriage or station in a state of intoxication, or committing any nuisance, or willfully interfering with the comfort of other passengers, and every person obstructing any officer of the company in the discharge of his duty, is hereby subjected to a penalty not exceeding *five pounds*, and shall immediately, or if travelling, at the first opportunity, be removed from the company's premises, and forfeit his fare.

Sec. 10.—Any passenger cutting the linings, removing or defacing the number-plates, breaking the windows, or otherwise wilfully damaging or injuring any Carriage on the Railway, shall forfeit and pay a sum not exceeding *Fifty Pounds*, in addition to the amount of damage done.

Sec. 11.—No Gratuity is under any circumstances allowed to be received by the Company's Servants, and any person interfering with this regulation, by giving or promising any Gratuity, is hereby subjected to a Penalty not exceeding *Five Pounds*.

GOODHUGH & TREMBATH, PRINTERS, 48, FLINDERS LANE, EAST, AND 174, ELIZABETH STREET.

A time-table of the first steam train service in Australia was printed on satin and presented to the Governor, Sir Charles Hotham, at the opening ceremony in Melbourne on 12 September 1854

THE FIRST SCREAM!

RAILWAYS WON THE ARGUMENT against canals, and a "navigation canal" has never been dug in Australia. As the first permanent way for a steam train was laid between Melbourne and Williamstown, the pride and excitement of the citizens grew with every foot of rail. When the driving-wheels turned at last, the Melbourne *Argus* of 12 September 1854 exulted that: "At length the iron horse starts fairly on its mission in Australia. The inauguration of the Hobson's Bay Railway will be a memorable event in the annals of the antipodes, and the 12th September will henceforth be appropriately signalised in the calendar of Victoria. Though only 'a day of small things,' as regards the extent of the undertaking, it is pregnant with interest as the initiatory step in that grand career of material progress, which has become the distinguishing characteristic of modern civilization. The shrill tones of the steam whistle will indicate to-day as significantly as if the cannon were booming in celebration of our independence that a new era has dawned upon us. The spirit of material progress is pre-eminently the spirit of the age; and without the aid of such cheap and quick communication as railways afford this progress cannot be realised.

"When we contemplate the future which the railway opens up to Australia, we may well hail with our loudest hurrahs, the great day in which we listen to 'the first scream!' We hear it today sounding across the busy, dusty flat, already worn with incessant traffic; but the scream of today is but the keynote to a thousand others, which will yet ring through many a wild hollow, awakening them all to life and usefulness. The time comes fast when it will sound over plain and hill, for many a mile away from present signs of civilization, scaring the wild animals from their repose, and warning them that their arch-enemy is upon them in earnest, at last. We look but a little into the future now, to foresee the train rushing through some region, at present utterly unknown. We see the wilddog, scared by such unwonted sight and sound, quicken his long sling trot into a frightened canter, as he leaves his light track upon the morning dew, and, with his head turned backward in a stealthy wonder at the fearful stranger, bounds off to his fastness in the ranges. We see the startled cattle run roaring to their camps; as like men, they need in their hours of danger, their public meetings and their parliaments: in which also like men, it too often happens, that the most senseless of the group makes the most fuss and roars the loudest. We see troops of our colonial steeds raise their heads inquisitively from their pastures, and, after one or two premonitory snorts, gallop off madly through the bush, with that wild, rushing, pattering sound which every bushman knows so well—their race half-play, half-terror.

"We see the train flash past the gunya of the native black. And as he greets the wonder with his own loud 'wah!' he, too, listens with a vague terror to the 'first scream.' Yes, listen, dusky fellow-subject, for there comes Christian England, the great, the powerful, the intelligent, the good! There comes Christian England, who if you were strong enough to demand a price for your land, would *buy* it of you, but who, as you are few and weak and timorous, generously condescends to *steal* it! There comes Christian England to absorb your hunting-grounds, destroy your game, inoculate you to her vices, and show her Christian spirit by dooming you to "extirpation!" There comes

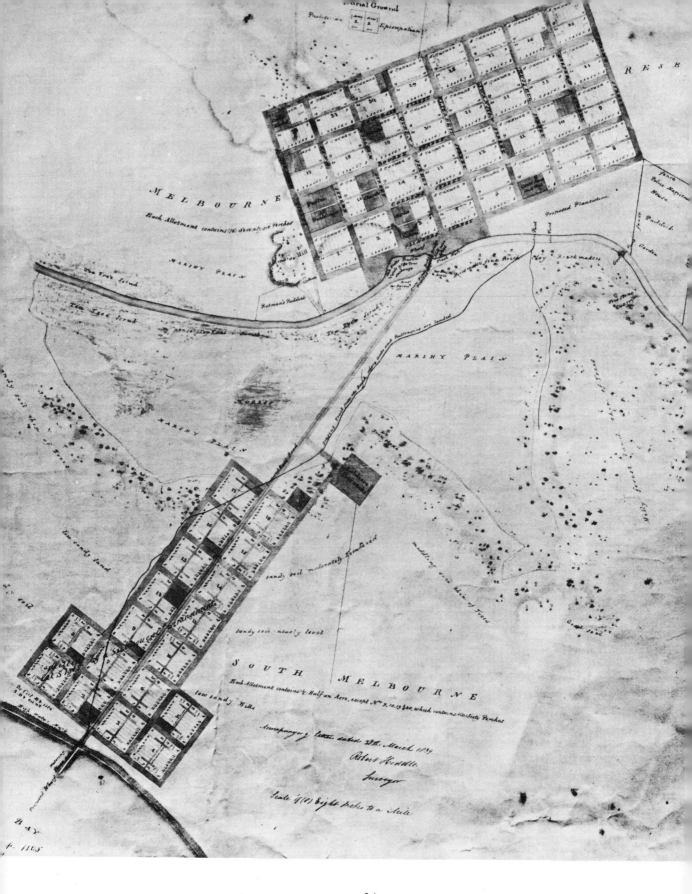

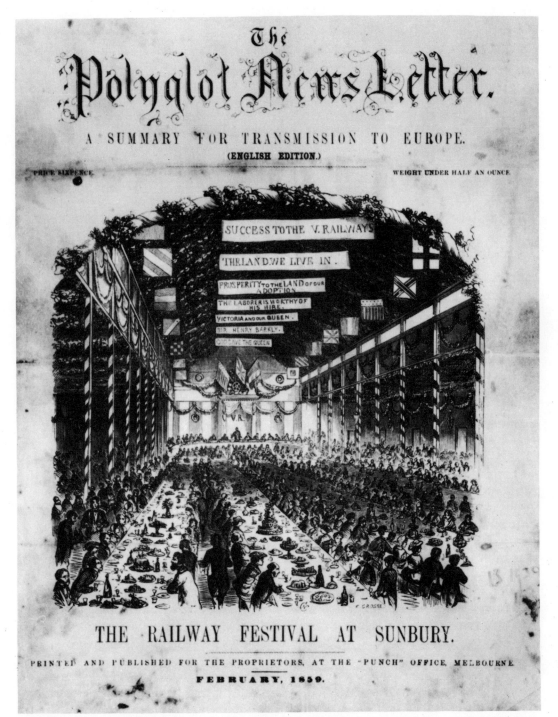

The Railway Festival at Sunbury.

Facing Page: *The first proposal for a railway in Victoria was accompanied by this plan, drawn by Robert Hoddle, Government Surveyor, in March 1839.*
Above: *A railway banquet of the 1850s, celebrating the opening of the line to Sunbury, Victoria*

The City Terminus of the M. & H.B. Railway Compy. 1854

Christian England, who carries many hundreds of tons of your gold without setting apart one ounce for you, who hands you over to be contaminated by the worst and lowest of her own people, to be taught their crimes, to be impregnated with their diseases, and who, while rapidly destroying you, cants in her churches and her religious meetings about doing to others as she would be done by! Rejoice, you dark-skinned savage, at the advent of your kind, magnanimous and most Christian brother!

"From the hut of the lone settler, too, we hear the impressive sound of the 'first scream.' We see him lay aside his short black pipe, shake up his vegetative faculties from the effects of strong tea, monotony, solitude, and tobacco, and with some toil and effort, once more endeavour to elaborate an idea. We see him gaze vacantly before him as the shrill whistle sounds more and more faintly in the distance, and we inwardly pray that he be brought to see the error of his ways; to repent of the desolation which he has so long caused by persistence in his odious monopoly; to reflect that the scores of miles of land over which he extends his sway, are fit for some better purpose than he has ever put them to; are capable of being turned to a higher use than being tottered over by a handful of his scabby sheep.

"The opening of the first railway is a suggestive topic, but we must put a check upon the visions which present themselves. We trust most sincerely that this first experiment may be a successful one, and that its results, even in money profits, may induce still further enterprise in a similar direction, amongst our monied men. We confess that we do not admire the sort of sandwich-and-table beer style of celebration of this great national event, which has found favour in the eyes of the directors. We believe, on the contrary, that nothing is lost, but that a good deal is gained, by giving due prominence to great occasions like this, and by infusing a dash of geniality into all our most important business undertakings. While we say this, however, we shall feel as warm an interest as any colonist in Victoria in the success of the Hobson's Bay Railway. We shall be delighted to find that it goes on and prospers. We hail this as a happy day, not only for Victoria, but for Australia, and we can prognosticate nothing but happy results from a fortunate combination of the 'iron horse' and the 'Hotham spur.' "

Next day the paper had to eat its sour comments upon the "sandwich-and-table beer style of celebration," for the whole occasion was carried off with immense gusto and the banquet provided for invited guests was a real blow-out. On 13 September 1854, under the heading, INAUGURATION OF THE MELBOURNE & HOBSON'S BAY RAILWAY, the newspaper reported, "Yesterday was memorable in the annals of Victoria and of Australia, for the opening of the first Australian Railway.

"One second-class and two first-class carriages were in attendance, for the conveyance of the guests. They were handsomely painted and varnished, and very commodious, but the locomotive attracted more of the attention of the bystanders. It is the first locomotive constructed, not merely in Victoria, but in the southern

Facing page: *The city terminus of the Melbourne and Hobson's Bay Railway Company, sketched in 1854.*

Below: *The opening of the Geelong and Melbourne Railway, 25 June 1857. Spencer Street Station was the terminus for this line*

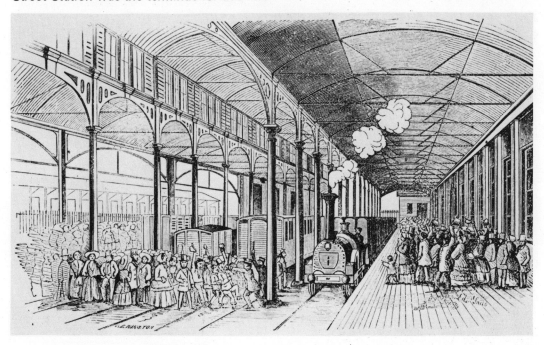

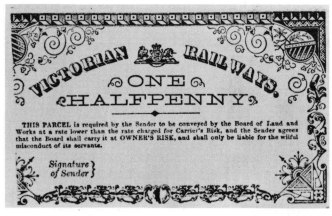

Above: *An early parcels stamp. Carriage of parcels has always been a function of Australian railways.* Right: *A tender for earthworks on an early New South Wales' line. Railways in that State were the first Government-owned railway system in the British Empire*

TENDER *for Works on the Hunter River Railway between Newcastle and Hexham.*

I, *William Wright* of *Sydney*

hereby tender to execute certain Works, viz.: Earthwork, Fencing, Clearing, Brickwork, Masonry, Carpentry, and Ironwork; at the Rates shewn in the following Schedule of Prices; and I submit the following persons, viz.:—

William Randle, Contractor, Sydney

and ~~~~ as my securities to ~~the amount~~ *any amount* ~~that~~ *the Directors* *may require* for the due execution of the Works.

I also agree to enter into a Bond for the due execution of this Contract when called upon to do so by the Directors.

SCHEDULE OF PRICES

Referred to in the foregoing Tender.

	£	s.	d.
Price for EXCAVATION taken out of the Cuttings, and deposited in the Banks, according to the form and dimensions shewn in the drawings			
In Clay or Sand deposited at any distance not exceeding 30 yards, per cubic yard		2	11
Price for Excavation deposited at any distance, not exceeding 20 chains			
Excavation in Clay or Sand, per cubic yard		3	9
Ditto in Ironstone Clay or Shale per cubic yard		4	6
Ditto in Sandstone Rock, per cubic yard		9	0
Additional Prices for carriage beyond ¼ mile, not exceeding ½ mile per cubic yard			
Ditto, not exceeding ¾ mile per cubic yard			3
Ditto, 1 mile			9
Price for Clearing Land from Timber and Scrub, per acre	8	0	0
Price for 3 rail Ironbark Fencing of the best description, per rod		15	0
4 Rail Ironbark Fencing, per rod		17	0
5 Feet Ironbark Paling Fence,		15	0
6 Feet ditto ditto	2	5	0
BRICKWORK in Mortar, for Bridges and Culverts per cubic yard	4	5	0
Ditto, in Cement,	5	5	0
MASONRY.			
Coursed Rubble Masonry, per cubic yard	4	15	0
Ashlar Masonry, per cubic foot		4	0
Fine Dressed Ashlar, in String Courses, Coping, &c., per cubic foot		10	0

TIMBERWORK.	£	s.	d.
Ironbark Beams and Framing, fixed complete, large scantlings, per cubic foot		6	0
Ironbark in small scantlings, fixed complete, per cubic foot		8	0
Ironbark Sawn Planking, fixed			
4 Inch thick, per cubic foot		8	0
3 Inch ditto ditto		8	6
2 Inch ditto ditto		9	6
1 Inch ditto ditto		9	
Baltic or Oregon Pine fixed small scantlings, per cubic foot			
Planking fixed			
4 Inch thick per cubic foot		7	0
3 Inch ditto ditto		7	6
2 Inch ditto ditto		8	0
1 Inch ditto ditto		8	6
PILING.			
Ironbark Piles shod with wrought Iron Shoes of 45 lb. each, and driven complete			
10 to 15 feet long, per cubic foot		10	0
15 to 40 feet long, per cubic foot		9	6
IRONWORK.			
Wrought Iron in Bolt			10
Straps, Nuts, &c., per pound		1	2

Signature *William Wright*
5th October 1854

NOTE.—Net Measurements only will be allowed in Estimating quantities of Work done.

hemisphere. It is the work of Messrs Robertson, Martin, Smith & Co., and was completed in ten weeks. It is six-wheeled, with a tubular boiler, and the tender is on the same body as the engine. The engine is only 30 h.p. and its power of traction is equal to 130 tons at a speed of 25 miles per hour. The appearance of both locomotive and carriages seemed to give general satisfaction.

"Shortly after 12 o'clock, His Excellency, the Lieutenant Governor and Lady Hotham arrived, and were received at the Station by William Nicholson, Esq. M.L.C. Chairman of Directors, Mr Watson, Manager, and several Directors. Copies of the by-laws and of the time-table printed upon satin were presented to His Excellency. Sir Charles and Lady Hotham were then conducted to one of the carriages and the three carriages were speedily laden with their full complement. An open third-class carriage, next to the locomotive, contained the Band of the 40th Regiment.

"The first train on the new railway started at 20 minutes past twelve, amid the music of the band and the cheering and waving of hats of the innumerable spectators. Its progress was at an exceedingly slow pace, until the bridge over the Yarra had been crossed, and then it proceeded on to Sandridge at the rate of about 15 miles an hour. On arriving at Sandridge where the train was welcomed with a salute from the Bay, the passengers alighted and walked down the jetty which runs for some way into the Bay, or inspected the station and its environs.

"Sir Charles Hotham, we believe, occupied himself in inspecting the railway works there, and in examining the engineer on the subject. Two more passages were made by the train ere all the guests were at the scene of the banquet.

"The engine-shed—an enormous hall of zinc—was the place chosen for this entertainment [the banquet], and, as regards extent, no place could have been more suitable. It was handsomely decorated for the occasion with evergreens and flags. Three tables ran down the whole length of the room and a cross-table was placed at the upper end. The display set forth on these tables was an agreeable surprise to those who imagined that the affair was to be on the cheap and shabby system. The entertainment was, in every respect, a very handsome one. About three hundred ladies and gentlemen sat down to table. W. Nicholson, Esq. M.L.C. presided, having on his right hand, Sir Charles and Lady Hotham. At the cross-table were also seated the Acting Chief Justice Barry, Mr Justice Williams, the Colonial Secretary, the Attorney-General, the Speaker of the Legislative Council, the Collector of Customs, and several ladies. Dr Greeves, M.L.C., one of the Directors, acted as vice-president. In the body of the room we observed John O'Shanassy, M.L.C., H. Langlands, George Annand, M.L.C., Colonel Valliant, Captain Kaye, Captain Guiness of the *Fantome*, the Surveyor-General, Thomas Dickson, and many of our leading citizens. Due justice having been done to the sumptuous viands, the more interesting part of the entertainment commenced.

"The Chairman said that the toast he had to propose was one always received with applause by the Briton—it was 'The Queen,' drunk with three times three, [to the music of] 'God Save the Queen.'

"The Chairman then proposed Prince Albert and the rest of the Royal Family. The toast was drunk with applause, [to the music of] 'Prince Albert's March.'"

OPENING OF THE RAILWAY TO TAMWORTH,

1. ROASTING THE BULLOCK—GENERAL FESTIVITIES.   2. THE VICE-REGAL TRAIN—BULLOCKS VERSUS STEAM.   3. GATHERING TO WELCOME THE GOVERNOR AND MINISTERIAL PARTY TO TAMWORTH.

The banquet set the pattern for the opening of every Australian railway after that. It started a gastronomic binge from coast to coast, north to south. Railways were the millennium come in our time, and the way to show our delight and pride was in a real slap-up spread.

At the opening of the Geelong–Melbourne rail on 25 June 1857, "when the engine astonished residents by a peculiarly harmonious whistle," the guests sat down to two and three-quarter tons of poultry, two and three-quarter tons of meats, three-quarters of a ton of fish, three-quarters of a ton of pastries, half a ton of jellies and ices, half a ton of fruit, a ton of bread, and unlimited wines, spirits and ales.

However, this feast was a perfect fiasco; a nightmare of the type which haunts all officialdom when planning a grand occasion. On 25 June 1857, under the heading OPENING OF THE GEELONG AND MELBOURNE RAILWAY the *Argus* gleefully reported: "The *Citizen* Steamer heavily laden, to the number of 4 or 5 hundred, left the Queen's Wharf about 11 o'clock a.m. and arrived shortly before 12 o'clock at the temporary pier, adjacent to the temporary station, erected in a stony meadow. Upon this temporary station a considerable quantity of bunting was displayed and a number of the water police officiated as special constables, and vigilantly preserved the platform from the intrusive footsteps of the visitors.

"Shortly after 12 o'clock a wreath of white smoke was discerned in the distance, an agitated bellman commenced stunning the ears of the bystanders, an itinerant band struck up 'God Save the Queen,' and half a thousand shivering people made preparations to take their places on the coming train. To the dismay of the expectants, the train seemed to be full of people from Geelong, most of whom thrust their head from the windows of the carriages, and appeared to regard in a singular mixture of wonder and pity, the assembled multitude. The Governor, the Chief Secretary, and other notabilities, were in one of the carriages, and alighted in a few moments, for the purpose, apparently, of inspecting the station or the township, both of which could be comprehensively surveyed at a glance; and his Excellency unhesitatingly resumed his seat almost immediately and preparations were made for returning. Some little delay occurred, owing to the restiveness of the engine, and this having been overcome, another difficulty was experienced in consequence of the combined inability of the carriages and disability of the locomotive. By the aid, however, of a physical force demonstration, got up by a portion of the 500 expectants, this was overcome, and the train proceeded on its way, leaving the visitors from Melbourne in the state of blank amazement. By 1 o'clock symptoms of hunger manifested themselves on the part of those who had been invited to a distant déjeuner, and a good many persons hastened down to the *Citizen* and appeased the pangs of their appetites with such provender as was attainable. The Cabinet Minister was observed from the vessel, rejoicing in the acquisition of a goodly slice of bread and cheese, while many individuals were observed ruefully conning an advertisement setting forth the number of tons, hundredweight, quarters and pounds of poultry included in 'Hooper's Bill of Fare.' The weary hours crept past, during which the company remained 'sub frigido,' the ladies shivering, and the gentlemen sw----- and occasionally debating the propriety of an indignation meeting. Dreary clouds discharged their dreary showers upon the dreary landscape,

The pageantry of railways often included the ceremony of turning the first sod on a new line. Here the Great Southern Railway, Western Australia, starts off with great pomp and style at Beverley in October 1886

while the faces of the spectators wore a drearier aspect than either the clouds or the scenery, nor was this dreariness altogether dispelled by the appearance about 2 o'clock of a train of empty carriages, which were dropped by the engine in the midst of an accumulation of viscid and adhesive mud, through which ladies had to pick their way, and over which the patent leather boots of military volunteers made a profound impression. At length the whole of the 500 shivering and hungry company were seated and a start was effected at about the same time that the dinner was appointed to commence at Geelong. The train proceeded slowly and cautiously over the newly ballasted line, and after reaching the main line the speed was increased and the action, though pretty rapid, was smooth enough. The greatest speed attained, however, (judging from experience) did not exceed 28 to 30 miles per hour. The nature of the country through which the line passes needs very little description.

"The train started at five past two and stopped at Geelong terminus at five past four having taken two hours to accomplish the distance (43 miles). How the people waiting at the other end of the line were circumstanced we know not. One of the locomotive Superintendents, on the engine that first came down in the morning, fell and was dreadfully injured. The accident took place near Geelong and the unhappy sufferer immediately conveyed thither.

"On the arrival of the train at the platform, it was found to be crowded to excess with boys and men, who forced their way into the carriages, before the passengers got out in many instances. No one was stationed to indicate the way to the scene of the festivities, which was very tortuous. On the arrival of the Melbourne guests the dinner was over.

"It would be difficult to produce a greater failure than the whole affair was, as far as those invited from Melbourne were concerned, or a more discreditable scheme of management.

"His Excellency the Governor rose immediately after the entrance of the Melbourne guests. Very few of his remarks were audible as those who had refreshed themselves, crowded around him closely. Had this not been the case, the confusion prevailing both inside and outside must have prevented his being distinctly heard to say nothing of the frequent scream of the engine outside the window.

"As far as the decoration of the booking office in which the dinner took place was concerned, it was in good taste and the tables must have been very well laid out, but two hours make a difference in appearance when some 2,500 people have dined. Mr Walters, the Superintendent who met with the accident, died. The ball took place in the hall where the dinner was given. Every arrangement was made to render it a brilliant affair."

After that, scarcely a day passed without mention of railways in the daily papers. Openings of new lines were given a full page of drawings in the illustrated weeklies; mostly delightful, emotionally charged vignettes of a new nation surging forward. "Nothing can stop us now!" was the feeling of the day.

Among other results of the coming of the railways, the upsurge in printing was meteoric. Booklets, guides, timetables, rules and regulations, posters, warnings — and Bradshaw's.

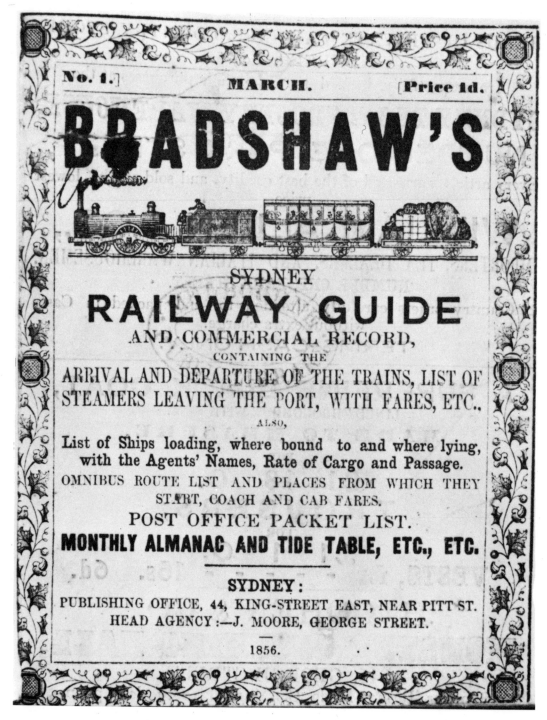

The cover of the first issue of Australia's Bradshaw's Railway Guide

BRADSHAW'S

As THE PUBLISHERS pointed out, *Bradshaw's Sydney Railway Guide* was "found in every public place." It was a "Commercial Record" according to them, but in fact was a newsy little information sheet ranging from advertisements for "A Superfine Black Coat—lined throughout with silk—made to measure for £1.18.0," to a Missing Friends column.

It contained information about the "Arrival and Departure of The Trains, List of Steamers Leaving the Port, with Fares etc., also, List of Ships loading, where bound to and where lying, with the Agents' Names, Rate of Cargo and Passage; Omnibus Route List and Places From which They Start, Coach and Cab Fares; Post Office Packet List, Monthly Almanac and Tide Table.".

George Bradshaw issued his first time-table in England in October 1839. By December 1842 he began a regular monthly publication, named, as was his later Australian time-table, *Bradshaw's Railway Guide*. It grew with the railways and in time the modest little folder became a huge tome. By 1865 the complications of *Bradshaw's* guide were so well known that *Punch* seized upon its notoriety and for eight weeks lampooned the daggers, asterisks, footnotes, abbreviations, and "see page so-and-so." Far from harming the greatest of all railway guides, the series of articles elevated *Bradshaw's* to the level of a national institution.

Even though the time-table in that first Sydney *Bradshaw's* is simple, the table of fares is as confusing as most travellers find those of the 1970s, but for entertainment there was nothing like the little book.

The first issue in March 1856 printed the "Bye-laws, Sydney Railway," the first clause of which read: "CONVEYANCE OF PASSENGERS—No passenger will be allowed to take his seat in or upon any of the railway carriages or to travel therein upon the railway, without having first paid his fare." The exhortations increase in volume and intensity from TICKETS TO BE SHEWN to DEFACING CARRIAGES. This latter warning is issued to "Any person who shall wilfully cut the linings, remove or deface the number-plates, or remove or extinguish any of the lamps in the carriages, break the windows or otherwise damage any of the railway carriages." The penalty would be five pounds for each offence, as well as payment for the damage itself. Five pounds was also the penalty for neglecting SHUTTING GATES UPON LINE as soon as person and "carriage, cattle, or animals under his charge have passed through the same." But for OBSTRUCTING ENGINE OR CARRIAGES "wilfully" they offered "ten years imprisonment with or without hard labour."

It was first on, first served according to Clause 3, for "Passengers at Intermediate Stations can only be booked conditionally, that is to say, in case there shall be room in the train in which they are booked. In case there shall not be room in the train for all the passengers booked, those booked for the longest distance shall have the preference; and those booked for the same distance shall have priority according to the order in which they are booked."

SMOKING was "strictly prohibited, both in and upon the Carriages, and in the

SYDNEY RAILWAY—Down Trains.

Through Trains.
* For Extra Trains to NEWTOWN, see page 8.

Dist.	STATIONS.	DAILY TRAINS—1st, 2nd, and 3rd Class.						Sunday Trains.		
Miles.	LEAVE—	a.m.	a.m.	a.m.	noon.	p.m.	p.m.	a.m.	p.m.	p.m.
0	SYDNEY......	6·0	8·0	10·0	12·0	3·0	5·15	9·0	3·0	6·0
	ARRIVE AT—									
2	NEWTOWN ...	6·7	8·7	10·7	12·7	3·7	5·22	9·7	3·7	6·7
5	ASHFIELD ...	6·15	8·15	10·15	12·15	3·15	5·30	9·15	3·15	6·15
6½	BURWOOD ...	6·21	8·21	10·21	12·21	3·21	5·36	9·21	3·21	6·21
7¾	HOMEBUSH..	6·27	8·27	10·27	12·27	3·27	53.4	9·27	3·27	6·27
13¼	Parramatta...	6·42	8·42	10·42	12·42	3·42	5·57	9·42	3·42	6·42

SYDNEY RAILWAY—Up Trains.

Through Trains.

Dist.	STATIONS.	DAILY TRAINS—1st, 2nd, and 3rd Class.						Sunday Trains.		
Miles.	LEAVE—	a.m.	a.m.	a.m.	p.m.	p.m.	p.m.	a.m.	p.m.	p.m.
0	Parramatta...	7·0	9·0	11·0	2·0	4·0	6·15	10·0	4·0	7·0
	ARRIVE AT—									
5¾	HOMEBUSH..	7·15	9·15	11·15	2·15	4·15	6·30	10·15	4·15	7·15
7	BURWOOD...	7·21	9·21	11·21	2·21	4·21	6·36	10·21	4·21	7·21
8½	ASHFIELD ...	7·27	9·27	11·27	2·27	4·27	6·42	10·27	4·27	7·27
11½	NEWTOWN ...	7·36	9·36	11·36	2·36	4·36	6·51	10·36	4·36	7·36
13¼	SYDNEY......	7·42	9·42	11·42	2·42	4·42	6·57	10·42	4·42	7·42

TABLE OF FARES FOR PASSENGERS.

FROM.	SYDNEY.			NEWTOWN.			ASHFIELD.			BURWOOD.			HOMEBUSH.			PARRAMATTA		
	CLASSES			CLASSES			CLASSES			CLASSES			CLASSES			CLASSES		
	1	2	3	1	2	3	1	2	3	1	2	3	1	2	3	1	2	3
	s. d.	s. d.	s. d.	s. d.	s. d.	s. d.	s. d.	s. d.	s. d.	s. d.	s. d.	s. d.	s. d.	s. d.	s. d.	s. d.	s. d.	s. d.
SYDNEY	—	—	—	0·9	0·6	0·3	2·0	1·3	0·9	2·6	1·9	1·0	3·0	2·0	1·3	3·6	2·6	1·6
NEWTOWN...	0·6	0·4	0·3	—	—	—	1·6	1·0	0·9	1·6	1·0	0·9	2·0	1·6	0·9	3·3	2·3	1·8
ASHFIELD....	2·0	1·3	0·9	1·6	1·0	0·9	—	—	—	1·0	0·9	0·6	1·6	1·0	0·9	2·9	2·0	1·0
BURWOOD...	2·6	1·9	1·0	1·6	1·0	0·9	1·0	0·9	0·6	—	—	—	1·0	0·9	0·6	2·3	1·9	1·0
HOMEBUSH..	3·0	2·0	1·3	2·0	1·6	0·9	1·6	1·0	0·9	1·0	0·9	0·6	—	—	—	2·0	1·6	0·9
Parramatta...	3·6	2·6	1·6	3·3	2·3	1·3	2·9	2·0	1·0	2·3	1·9	1·0	2·0	1·6	0·9	—	—	—

CHARGES FOR DOGS AND PARCELS.

FROM.	Dogs.	Parcels.		Dogs.	Parcels.		Dogs.	Parcels.		Dogs.	Parcels.		Dogs.	Parcels.		Dogs.	Parcels.	
	s. d.	14 lb	28 lb	s. d.	14 lb	28 lb	s. d.	14 lb	28 lb	s. d.	14 lb	28 lb	s. d.	14 lb	28 lb	s. d.	14 lb	28 lb
SYDNEY ...	—	—	—	0·6	0·3	0·6	0·9	0·6	1·0	0·9	0·6	1·0	1·0	0·9	1·6	1·6	1·0	2·0
NEWTOWN.	0·6	0·3	0·6	—	—	—	0·6	0·3	0·6	0·9	0·6	1·0	0·9	0·6	1·0	1·6	1·0	2·0
ASHFIELD...	0·9	0·6	1·0	0·6	0·3	0·6	—	—	—	0·6	0·3	0·6	0·9	0·6	1·0	1·0	0·9	1·6
BURWOOD...	0·9	0·6	1·0	0·9	0·6	1·0	0·6	0·3	0·6	—	—	—	0·6	0·3	0·6	0·9	0·9	1·6
HOMEBUSH.	1·0	0·9	1·6	0·9	0·6	1·0	0·9	0·6	1·0	0·6	0·3	0·6	—	—	—	0·9	0·9	1·6
Parramatta..	1·6	1·0	2·0	1·0	1·0	1·9	1·0	0·9	1·6	0·9	0·9	1·6	0·9	0·9	1·6	—	—	—

TABLE OF FARES—CONTINUED.

CHILDREN above THREE and under TEN YEARS of age. half the fares will be charged.

PASSENGERS travelling by FIRST-CLASS CARRIAGES will be allowed to take with them 100 lbs. weight of Personal Luggage. (Free of Charge.)

Ditto, travelling by SECOND-CLASS CARRIAGES will be allowed to take with them 60 lbs. weight of Personal Luggage. (Free of Charge.)

Ditto, travelling by THIRD-CLASS CARRIAGES will be allowed to take with them 40 lbs. weight of Personal Luggage. (Free of Charge.)

Extra Luggage will be charged at the rate of 1s. 6d. (One Shilling and Sixpence) per cwt. for the whole distance and proportionate rates for Intermediate Distances.

N.B.—No responsibility will be taken by the Railway for Luggage, unless it be specially Booked and Paid for. Passengers are particularly requested their Names and Destination marked on their Luggage, and to see it deposited in the Train. Goods or Packages, of any description, not coming fairly under the denomination of "Luggage," will be liable to the ordinary Parcel Rates.

HORSES and CARRIAGES must be at the Station not later than 15 minutes before the Time named for the departure of the Train by which they are intended to be sent. To prevent disappointment, six hours previous notice should, if possible, be sent to the Station Master.

RATES FOR HORSES AND CARRIAGES.

For 1 Horse, 7s. ; 2 Horses, 6s. each ; 3 Horses and any greater number, 5s. each. For each 4-wheeled

Above and facing page: Time-tables and fares from the first issue (March 1856) of Bradshaw's Sydney Railway Guide.

Advertisements from Bradshaw's Sydney Railway Guide *provide an interesting background to the birth of the age of steam*

Stations." There were penalties for WALKING ON THE LINE, INTOXICATION, and OBSTRUCTING RAILWAY OFFICIALS; and warnings against offering FEES TO PORTERS who were not permitted to accept them.

The almanac for March 1856 reminds the traveller that on the third day of the month, the previous year, Emperor Nicholas died; that High Water at Sydney would be at 5.42; and gardeners should sow winter tares, cape barley, mangel-wurzel, and wheat. They should "dress vines" and were told that "raisin and sweet wines may be made."

Times are given for RAILWAY OMNIBUSES that "meet the trains" and "await the arrival of each train," charge three pence each person and take parcels as well.

Blocks of information are crammed around railway notices and advertisements. RULES OF THE SYDNEY EXCHANGE ROOM are jammed between SHIPS FROM MELBOURNE and an IMPORTANT NOTICE which gives the number of the bank notes "which were in the Mail-bag lost between Brisbane and Ipswich." The public is cautioned that payment is stopped on these notes. The sub-head under IMPORTANT NOTICE tells us in italics that "Parties wishing to Advertise for their Friends can do so, free of charge, by forwarding the particulars to *Bradshaw's Sydney Railway Guide*."

> If Mr James Turpin of Melbourne or elsewhere, late of 23 Trinity Terrace, Borough, London, will write to the Editor of *Bradshaw's Sydney Railway Guide* he will hear from a friend he left in England ("old motto, ask old Browne.")

There are fifteen requests to find missing friends. Miss Marion Peacock, if she replied, would hear from "an old school-fellow;" Mr Brown of the yacht *Wanderer* would hear from "an old chum;" and Mrs Lawley of Hobart Town would hear from her niece, Emma.

The advertisements are a cross section of the commercial life of Sydney in the days when the iron horse was a foal. Essence of Jamaica Ginger and Chamomile Flowers is recommended for flatulence and nervous affections; "Best Chilian Flour from the province of Concepcion by a line of clipper ships" will be supplied in any quantity not less than half a ton; the Church of England advertises Life Assurance under the patronage of the Lord Bishops of Sydney, Newcastle, Melbourne, Tasmania, and Adelaide (all the Bishops the church had at that time in Australia). A "Bird Stuffer" offers his services, a gentleman advertises Peruvian guano, and this feature appears: "Ourang Outang, Wild Man of the Woods, Boa Constrictor etc., being exhibited daily at No. 30 Hunter Street, Sydney."

Later issues expanded to include new features such as lists of unclaimed letters at the G.P.O., newspapers and periodicals in the Australian colonies, and Fares for Boatman Plying in the Harbour of Port Jackson. In fact, the little pocket-sized guide had more than enough reading matter to entertain the traveller for the distance then available for travel by train.

The *New South Wales Railway Guide* (official) could literally charm a traveller on to a train, and its wares were true to label. A sort of early days tourist brochure, it extolled the beauties and availability of the countryside.

The Australian gold rushes had started five years previous to this advertisement appearing in Bradshaw's

By 1879, when the hard-won fight to cross the Blue Mountains was well over, they were offering: "Route No. 4—From Sydney to Wentworth Falls (formerly called the Weatherboard Platform): 62 miles.—Should you desire to go from Sydney direct to 'The Weatherboard Gorge and the Campbell Cataract'—a grand piece of scenery of wondrous wildness and unrivalled beauty—your better way will be to drop a line by post to the keeper of the accommodation house at the 'Weatherboard,' Mr Charles Abraham Wilson; and having so arranged for your bed and entertainment, go up by the evening mail train and sleep. You will arrive at Mr C. A. Wilson's in the evening at about quarter past 11 o'clock. But whether you go up in the morning or in the evening, you must remember to tell the guard, at the old Blue Mountains station, to set you down at 'Wentworth Falls,' or you will be carried on to Mount Victoria. The accommodation house, a clean but unpretentious little place, stands close to where the train stops, and on the southern side of the line. Having slept there that night, you can, without fatigue, visit the Weatherboard Gorge and Cataract early on the following morning."

They knew the routes they extolled. "Take the morning train if you wish to see the varied scenery along the line on the Blue Mountains," they advertised for Route 1. "Particularly that of the First Zig-Zag near Emu Plains, and the Great Zig-Zag near Lithgow." On Route 2 they knew the tricks: "Come provided with a rug to sleep in between Bathurst and Orange."

Favouring none, but knowing all, they recommend on Route 6: "There is at Hartley, near the two churches, a decent, old fashioned, way-side inn, kept by Mrs Evans, the air being very bracing and remarkably pleasant, is much recommended for invalids." Every side excursion possible is mentioned: "Mount Victoria will be for you a good headquarters, from which Govett's Leap, at Blackheath, may conveniently be visited either by driving up to the eastward on the old road in a buggy, or by riding on a hired horse, or by walking along near the railway. The distance from Mount Victoria to Blackheath is only 4 miles, and the old road here is in a state of good repair."

The guide is as friendly and garrulous as the guides they had provided at most of their recommended beauty spots. "Route 5—From Sydney to Blackheath (i.e. 'Govett's Leap'): 73 miles.—If you should desire to pay a hasty visit to the lovely and stupendous gorge and waterfall usually known by the curiously inexpressive name of 'Govett's Leap' (and you do not particularly care whether you see any other spot on the occasion or not), take your place in the train for Blackheath, and tell the guard at 'The Blue Mountains' (or Lawson station) to put you down at Blackheath. There is a convenient accommodation house here, 2 miles from Govett's Leap, on the north side of the line; an easy walk, and an easy way to find. You had better sleep at the inn, and return to Sydney on the next day by the 'up' train; for Blackheath is only a siding with a platform, and you may find it troublesome to be up and ready at the proper time so to get to Sydney by the eight train from Bathurst and Orange. If you find yourself comfortable at Blackheath, and time permits, you can ride, drive, or walk thence to Mount Victoria and back."

The front cover of the six-page Railwayiana, published in Tasmania, portrays the "Seer's Warning" on the effects of railways on the State

RAILWAYIANA

EVEN BEFORE THEY had heard "The First Scream" or the "peculiarly harmonious whistle," Tasmania had produced a six-page publication, *Railwayiana*, price six pence. The storm in the brain of Philip Fysh, then standing for the Legislative Council, it lampoons several figures in the island state that has never been gentle on its own sons. As if that wasn't enough, Tasmania shortly afterwards published a *Railway Songster* in which they broke out in verses "suitable to be sung on trains." Songs like, "She danced like a fairy, and sang like a bird; She did, on my word, but rather absurd, she doated on Harwood, a man you have heard, And so she skedaddled from me." And there is "Don'ts you Touch my Girl": "Keep your maulers off of Sal, I don't allow you to touch my gal, Hit me, Smash me, knock me down, But don't you touch my gal."

The publishers anticipated lively times as the trains rattled onwards, but the apple island anthem of the day was "The Launceston And Deloraine Railway," sung to the tune "Marching Through Georgia."

Oh, hear the Railway whistle boys: it's notes are shrill and clear;
Just jump into the carriage, sir, there's nothing you may fear,
And let your voice re-echo as you shout it through the air,
The Launceston and Deloraine Railway.

CHORUS:
Hurrah! Hurrah! for the men that worked so hard,
Hurrah! Hurrah! for I'm the Railway Guard,
You'd like to know the stoker, so I have brought his card,
On the Launceston and Deloraine Railway.

The farmers they will bless them when they hear the joyful sound,
Of the Launceston and Western rolling o'er the ground;
And the native youths, God bless them, some work at last have found,
On the Launceston and Deloraine Railway.

CHORUS:
Hurrah! Hurrah! for the men that sets us free—
Hurrah! Hurrah! for Mr Adye D.
A reserved seat we'll always keep for Mr Johnny C.,
On the Launceston and Deloraine Railway.

Oh, yes, we'll keep a seat for them, and Mr Norwood too,
And others who were friends to us shall bear the flag of blue;
And England when we sent to her she found us all the screw,
For the Launceston and Deloraine Railway.

CHORUS:

> *Hurrah! Hurrah! for the horse that goes by steam;*
> *Hurrah! Hurrah! for the Railway whistle's scream.*
> *The people down in Hobarton can use the four-horse team*
> *While we go to Deloraine by Railway.*

They gave us lots of trouble, boys, before we passed the Bill;
The main line was a bubble boys, our fondest hopes to kill;
But now they've got the double boys, although against their will,
By the Launceston and Deloraine Railway.

CHORUS:

> *Hurrah! Hurrah! the Debentures they are sold,*
> *Hurrah! Hurrah! for the use of England's gold,*
> *For soon we will repay them and those that shares do hold*
> *By the Launceston and Deloraine Railway.*

But soon they sent to us to sign their Railway policy,
And sent them back already filled to Mr Charles To-be;
Why don't they get a man to work like our Sir Richard D.,
For their Main Trunk Railway.

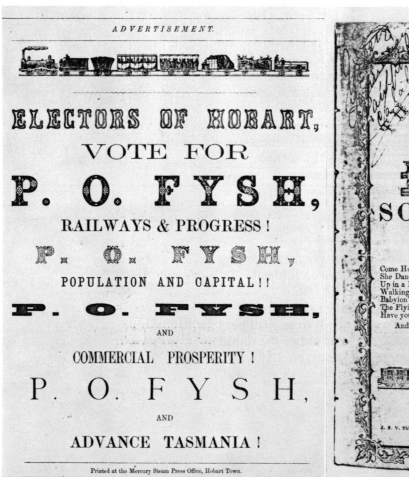

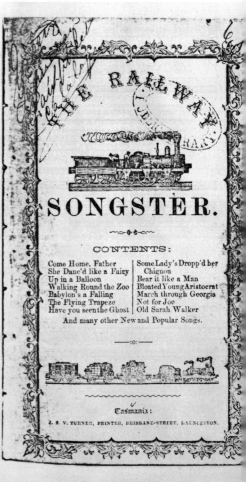

CHORUS:

Hurrah! Hurrah! the Trunk is all my eyes;
Hurrah! Hurrah! do you know the reason why?
They hav'nt got the men to work like Dowling, Crookes, and Dry,
For the great Shoe Trunk Railway.

Tenders have been accepted, and the work will soon begin,
And soon we'll feel the benefit of the Melbourne Company's tin:
Yes, every shop in Launceston good stock must now lay in,
For the Launceston and Deloraine Railway.

CHORUS:

Hurrah! Hurrah! for Overend and Robb,
Hurrah! Hurrah! for soon they'll do the job,
And Launceston will soon be filled with people—such a mob;
For the Launceston and Deloraine Railway.

So let's return our thanks to them who love the native youths.
And who, to gain some work for them, have stood such vile abuse,
But crowned their efforts with success, which soon we will adduce
By the Launceston and Deloraine Railway.

CHORUS:

Hurrah! Hurrah! for the men who helped us through;
Hurrah! Hurrah! for the gallant Railway crew!
And every one whose motto is the never fading blue
And the Launceston and Deloraine Railway.

Another famous Tasmanian song was sung by Mr J. H. Melvyn at the opening of the Launceston and Deloraine in 1871, "the accompaniment embracing imitations of the noise of the railway train, and the shriek of the whistle."

PHILLIS ON THE RAILWAY

Will you come with me my Phillis dear
Down to the old Tamar's side
And we'll get on the railway
To Deloraine we'll ride!
All other countries go by steam.
They'll soon trip up our heels
We must have something faster dear
Than our old wagon wheels.

When everyone had wagons love
And travelled like a snail
We kept our place in commerce then,
But now we want the rail
I think the line will go ahead,
And prove a first-rate job,
Which will be a feather in the cap
Of Overend and Robb [the contractors].

Folks said it would take seven years
Before the works would end,
Do you believe it Phillis dear,
With Robb and Overend?
We've received their hospitality,
Which was really bona fide
So we'll jump on the wagon
And we'll all take a ride.

The ground plan and front elevation for the Maryborough (Victoria) Railway Station, for which tenders were called in March 1890

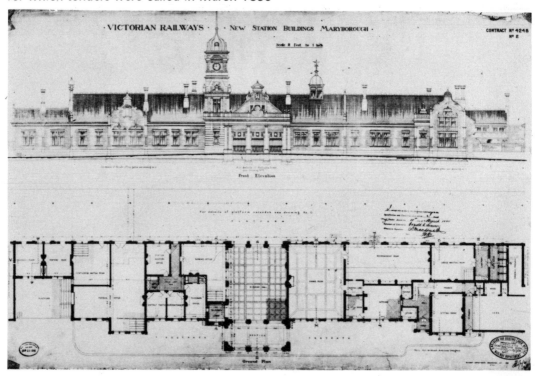

A STATION WITH TOWN ATTACHED

WHILE THE LONG WAIL of the whistle excited the countryside to break out in verse and the rails spread out suggesting mobility and adventure, the architecture that came with the trains brought a positive air of solidity and permanence. Much of the early architecture was among the best in the nation at that time. Often in the country, the railway buildings were the only fine constructions in the area.

The famous remark of Mark Twain at the close of the century that "Maryborough is a railway station with a town attached" was only a paraphrase of a quote from the 1891 *Victorian Railway Gazette* which asked "Where is Maryborough? Behind the railway station. This is the latest regarding that imposing monument, the Maryborough railway station, and those who have seen the gorgeous structure and taken notice of the comparative sizes of the borough and the station will readily perceive the meaning of the above."

Maryborough station still stands as a monument to its builders, and continues to lend distinction to the town. Many of the other architectural giants of their day have been dwarfed by time but their environmental suitability has not been superseded.

Some of the more attractive structures were built by the New South Wales railways, indeed, the same could be said of many of that State's outback railway stations as was said of Maryborough. In Bourke, the long low stone building in Dutch barn style has a simplicity and beauty that would be hard to better. Albury station, when it was built, was the most imposing in the State and still presents a pleasing appearance. The red and white bricks were brought from Belgium, and on its slate roof was built a seventy-two feet high clock tower. This imposing work could well have been done to impress the Victorians over the border who could clearly hear the train whistle long before the connection between the two States was made.

The platform at Albury is often mistakenly claimed to be Australia's longest, but at 1,497 feet is shorter than Flinders Street (Melbourne) with 2,097 feet, and Kalgoorlie (W.A.) with 1,730 feet. New South Wales went in for decorative cast iron lace work around its buildings, and on the line to Bourke and to Cobar are fine examples of it; even the Ladies and Gents signs are exquisitely wrought and most artistically satisfying.

Different styles were designed for different areas; there was no dull uniformity. One of the most delightful buildings was the mortuary platform in the heart of Sydney. From this Gothic building the trains left for the burial ground at Rookwood, where they pulled into a mortuary station. This building, with angels holding long trumpets bending low over the permanent way, ecclesiastical windows, spires, and bell tower, was presided over by a station master with white crepe ribbons round his black top hat and falling in a swathe down his back.

Far surpassing any other building work for environmental suitability, practicality, and aesthetic achievement (railmen would add) was the Great Zig-Zag. These massive earthworks and viaducts rival the Roman aqueducts, and were the means of getting trains over the Blue Mountains. Before plans were drawn up for this work the mountains had seemed impossible to cross by train. Suggestions had even been made that

Above: *Albury Railway Station, New South Wales, built from red and white bricks imported from Belgium, boasts a seventy-two foot clock tower.*
Centre: *An early painting of the original Perth Railway Station, Western Australia, c. 1881.*
Below: *The 1897 Perth Railway Station is still in use today*

Above: *Sydney Railway Station, New South Wales, in the 1870s*

Centre: *The Mortuary Station, Rookwood, New South Wales. This building was re-erected in 1958 in Canberra for use as a church.*
Below: *The Port Adelaide Railway Station, South Australia, c. 1868*

Above: *An early engraving of the railway bridge over St Kilda Road, used by the Melbourne, St Kilda, and Brighton Railway, Victoria.*
Below: *The Lithgow zig-zag, New South Wales, looking westwards. This masterpiece of engineering was opened in 1869*

passengers could be taken as far up the mountains as the gradient would allow a train to go, then they could walk up a staircase to the top of the mountain, and walk down a staircase to as far as a train could be taken on the other side.

When the Lithgow or Great Zig-Zag was built, it was regarded as one of the wonders of the world; visitors came from other countries to view this engineering masterpiece, and the countryside around it became one of the most popular picnicking spots from where its symmetrical viaducts and the entrances to its long tunnels were viewed.

All the colonists were interested in the work that was said "not to be surpassed by any railway in the world." The navvies complained that their worst obstacle, a 430-foot drop to the valley below, did not have footing even for a mountain goat. The surveyors had to be lowered over the mountainside on a rope, yet the engineers obtained a gradient of 1 in 33 at the extreme (a rise of one foot for every thirty-three feet forward travel). They blasted 85,000 tons of rock, "calling in the aid of electricity for the purpose," which was "successfully accomplished by galvanic agency, the electric spark having been communicated to the powder by the hand of the Countess of Belmore in the presence of his Excellency the Governor." A writer in 1869, journeying out to the just finished work wrote "of the pluck and enterprise of the colony of New South Wales in conceiving and carrying successfully through such a gigantic undertaking."

In 1926, half a century after the building of the zig-zag, New South Wales was again pioneering a "first" in railway architecture in Australia. To avoid the grades on the line from Kyogle to South Brisbane, they introduced a loop to gain altitude. This loop was the first of its kind in Australia and drew as much attention from the sight-seeing public as did the earlier architecture.

The extension of the standard gauge to Brisbane meant that passengers between the two States would be able to travel without changing trains. Two and a half miles on the New South Wales side of the border the line was raised sixty-five feet by incorporating a loop crossing over itself. Technically it was interesting: for 270 degrees, or three-quarters of a helix, the radius was constant at twelve chains.

When it was opened for traffic, passengers craned their necks to see the loop—they still do. And enthusiasts still walk the old route of the zig-zag (now by-passed), and a group is attempting to raise funds to put a train back on the old "roads" of the mountain-leveller.

In the sunshine of Queensland arcade-type protection was built over the stations and has become as much a part of the building scene in that State as the houses on stilts. Builders were left to decorate these arched verandahs as they wished and some are sculptured woodwork, others carved, a few cast iron filigree, and some as harsh as the harsh red land they are built on. Townsville station, with its great arch proclaiming "Great Northern Railway" is as colonial and tropical in atmosphere as anywhere in Australia, as redolent of the North as is Kuranda, the station almost entirely hidden by tropical plants.

Bridges vary from the great traditional spectacular to the bush-built timber criss-cross, each type suitable for its area. Gippsland, in the wet southern coast of Victoria,

Above: *The Picton Viaduct on the Great Southern Railway, New South Wales, as seen in 1866.*

Below: *A timber bridge, in the Gippsland area of Victoria, is in harmony with the virgin bush country*

Above: *The substantial Moorabool viaduct in Victoria*

Below: *The railway bridge across the Hawkesbury River, New South Wales*

Above: *The Picton tunnel on the Great Southern Railway, New South Wales, 1866.*
Facing page: *The city terminus of the Melbourne and Hobson's Bay Railway, Victoria—an S. T. Gill engraving c. 1854*

built wooden bridges across its forested hills that are still, today, visited as a spectacle of achievement. So too is the bridge over the Pieman River in Tasmania, a breath-catching span high over a wild river on the West Coast. Each State has its own individual architecture, each as fitting to their landscape as a rock jutting out of the ground, from lonely outposts on Eyre Peninsula (South Australia) to the sprawling isolated sidings on the way to Meekatharra (Western Australia). A State can almost be identified by its railway architecture.

Of course, this sudden surge of building and engineering works did not go unnoticed by the literary wits of the day. Tunnels in particular caught their imaginations. One wrote of the "Humours of Railway Tunnels": "To lovers, the railway tunnel is a regular paradise. These mortals can't always have an engaged compartment (they may not have a half-crown to spare, or the guard may not be able to find room) and even with this luxury they get scared at the whiz of passing stations (always seemingly crowded) and signalmen in their isolated boxes, which seem like rows of sentinels spying at them. The tunnel is, therefore, their favourite retreat.

"There are, however, tunnels short and tunnels long, and the latter may be subdivided into two classes, namely, kind and unkind. The short tunnel permits of only a squeeze of the hand. It is never thoroughly dark, and lovers are accordingly always on the alert. The long tunnel is more propitious and the impenetrable gloom generates courage. Arms, heads, and lips meet in the delicious obscurity, and fates get there and then sealed. The seconds of bliss appear to be spun out to years; the rattle of the wheels sounds like the raging world without; and the engine, as the train emerges into the light, crowns all with its uncouth scream, which says as plainly as can be, 'Bless you, my darlings!'

"Such is the kind tunnel; and now for its un-kind brother. It plays all sorts of pranks. There may be an opening in the roof shortly after entering it, which startles and gives distrust for the remainder of its course, or it may contain a series of ventilating shafts admitting the light of day; or, again, the sides of the tunnel may be studded with reflecting lamps. All this is very annoying. It looks as if done on purpose, and suchlike interference has spoilt many a good affair at the critical moment. But the glare from a passing train or the roar of a locomotive will play similar havoc.

"There is no doubt whatever about the supremacy of the long dark tunnel, and lines having a fair sprinkling of them along their route will find their dividends ascend by publishing the fact in their time-tables (and in large posters if desirable), stating, of course, the length and duration of the submerged journey, and the nature of the internal fittings in regard to roof holes and prying lights.

"Tricks are not infrequently played on these turtle-doves. A wag in a crowded compartment, on entering a tunnel, will chirp in an insinuating sort of way by placing his lips on the back of his hand to resemble a smack, and on emerging the embarrassment of the loving ones baffles all description. In fact, the blushes of the innocent pair will not have subsided for the next ten miles of the run."

The busy railway pier at Sandridge (Port Melbourne) about 1883. The old Port Phillip Bay steamship Edina *is on the left*

THE PACKHORSES OF THE NATION

FOR THE TRAVELLER, waiting on the station, the very sound of the engine taking its breath was enough to awe him, even humble him. John Ruskin wrote, "What manner of men they must be who dig brown ironstone out of the ground and forge it into *that*." The roar of the fire when the fireman swings in another shovel full of coal, the bark of the compressor, the sight of the wheels higher than a man's head, the mighty rods and cylinders beaten out with titanic hammer strokes into the precision of watchmaking, this infinitely complex anatomy of active steel some men even considered superior to the skeleton of a living creature.

But of all the senses, that of smell is the most abiding; tattooed on the olfactory nerves of those who grew up in the age of steam is the aroma of coal smoke, the very essence of excitement, adventure, travel, escape. To those who still scent the airs puffed out by this almost living thing, the steam locomotive was one of the finest sights on God's earth, the most splendid creation of the engineering faculties. Grown men could become completely enchanted with it. J. C. Rolland, one of the greatest rail buffs Australia has known, once carefully estimated that "an engine would emit on a 100 mile journey 96,000 puffs. Taking the running time at two hours, this would work out to 800 puffs a minute." To such extreme arithmetic did the greatest spinner of magic of all time send grown men.

In the recalling of their days of high summer, there is some parallel to the tales of the tall ships that disappeared even before steam engines did. Some engines spent their days on the glamour runs between the capital cities but many finished up as humble humdrum yard donkeys. A notable exception to this was the first Garratt to come to Australia.

Later the Garratts, with their characteristic "bark," would be the most widely known engine on Australian lines, but the first was a small, two foot gauge loco for Tasmania's West Coast mountain lines.

It is said that Garratt was a foreman in the London firm of Beyer Peacock, and one day, watching a locomotive boiler being taken along the rails by means of a trolley at either end, he got his idea. Why not a powerful locomotive with an engine chassis at each end?

At the time he put the idea before the company directors in London, the Tasmanian Government Railways, at the other end of the globe, were seeking a powerful locomotive for the two foot gauge of the steep grades and sharp curves of the North-East Dundas Railways. By 1911 two locomotives had been delivered, the first such in the world. These tough little mountaineers were famous for their feats on the Williamsford to Zeehan railway.

When the line closed, the locos were left unused in Zeehan, where Harold Williams, the Chief Engineer of Beyer Peacock, saw them on a visit in 1945. He bought the first built and had it shipped back to London where it now rests in the Beyer Museum.

The colonial boys had of course been building their own engines long before this. The Melbourne and Hobson's Bay Railway engineers had built not only their own

Above: *The first train on the Leonora to Gwalia line (Western Australia) in 1903. The double-decker carriages were designed for commuters between the twin goldfield towns.* Below: *The old "Sydney Express" being hauled in Victoria by A class locomotive No. 204 about 1910*

The "First Victorian" was assembled in 1862 from spare parts sent out with another engine from England. Foreman Barnes is standing on the front of the engine, and Enoch Chambers is standing on the right in the cab

Above: *The E class double-ender Fairlie locomotive, introduced in Western Australia in 1879.*
Below: *Katie, a C class locomotive, first introduced in Western Australia in 1881. The four-wheel tender was added in 1888, making a total weight of twenty-six tons*

ballasting engine but later, when the line was ready for traffic in 1854 and the locomotives had not arrived from England, they built their own in ten weeks. It was this
engine that hauled the first official train to run in Australia.

Later, in 1862, an engine named the "First Victorian" was built and this has always
caused a lot of dissension among Victorians who believe the little engine built in 1854
was the "First Victorian."

The building of this 1862 loco was described as late as 1904 in the *Australasian* by
Engineer R. Barnes. "Between the years 1855 and 1870, I was managing the engineering
business of the late Enoch Chambers. The works were in Little Collins Street, a little
way west of Swanston Street, and the office stood about where the Wesleyan Book-
room stands today. We had a large smith's shop and a good piece of ground at the back,
which was used as a boiler yard, and the fitting shop was a large iron building which
stood upon the ground now occupied by Messina & Co's printing office.

"We were a busy firm and in addition to our other business, we did a lot of work
for Cornish and Bruce, the contractors for what was then known as the Mount
Alexander and Murray River Railway. Soon after the contract was let, Cornish and
Bruce imported from Stephenson and Co. of Newcastle a locomotive for working
the ballast-trains and it was *No. 1378*. We were asked to take delivery and put it together.

"Cornish and Bruce, when importing the engine, got out with it a duplicate set of
wheels, axles and springs and a lot of spare tubes for the boiler. It was about April 1862
that Mr Chambers asked me if I thought we could, with these spares, build a similar
engine to the one in use as the contractors were much in need of another locomotive.
This, in addition to the work we had in hand, seemed a big undertaking to me.

"I had, however, at the time, a man working in the fitting shop named George Ogle,
a grand mechanic; he had been in the employ of Hawthorn & Co., the enginemakers
of Newcastle, and was a leading hand in the works at the time he came away. He was
quite familiar with Stephenson's 'Rocket' and often interested me in his description
of the way they used to reverse the gears before the invention of the link motion.

"So I talked the matter over of building the locomotive with Ogle. We came to
the conclusion with Ogle to become leading hand during its construction. The boiler
was at once put in hand and was made of the best Staffordshire plate, except the firebox
which was Low Moor iron. The frame plates gave us a lot of work. We went, however,
on a very safe line and copied '1378' in every way we possibly could and spared no
pains, and the result was when the engine was completed, it was a success, and was
named the 'First Victorian.' It took us much longer than was anticipated and it was the
latter part of 1862 before it was under steam. The engine weighed twenty tons and
when finished had to be put on the rails. This was done by taking it on its own wheels
down Little Collins Street to Spencer Street. A day or two after, steam was got up
for a trial run to Digger's Rest."

The honourable retirement and restoration of these early packhorses of a nation has
only begun in recent years, too late to save some of the most famous. The oldest to
survive and experience her moment of glory in Western Australia is "Katie," a fussy
old girl built by Robert Stephenson and Co. in Newcastle on Tyne in 1880 and in
service at Fremantle (W.A.) by 1881.

Above: *B class locomotive No. 4, placed in service on the South Australian Railways in 1856. It was converted to a tank engine in 1875, and then to a loco crane in 1893.*
Centre: *Locomotive No. 34, formerly known as the "Titania" on the Geelong and Melbourne Railway Company line, which opened on 25 June 1857.*
Below: *A timber tram locomotive used in the north-west of Tasmania, and built in 1885*

Above: *An industrial locomotive, "Peronne" was one of four purchased in 1919 by Broken Hill Associated Smelters Pty Ltd for use in the lead-smelting works at Port Pirie, South Australia.*

Below: *The "Leschenault Lady" is a vintage Western Australian train entirely renovated by volunteer labour under the direction of the Bunbury Tourist Bureau. Here it is being hauled by a G class locomotive, seen taking on water at Boyanup.*

Above: *A Commonwealth Railways NM class, introduced in 1925 for the "Ghan" on the Central Australia Railway. This class is similar to the Queensland Railways C17, of which 227 were put into service.*

Below: *One of four W class locomotives built for the Silverton Tramway Company, New South Wales, and based on the W class design of the Western Australian Government Railways, who used sixty of these locomotives for goods services.*

Above: *Tasmanian Railways M class No. 6 locomotive, repainted especially for the Centenary celebrations. Ten M class locomotives were placed in service, the first in 1951.*

Below: *A Western Australian S class Mountain type locomotive, stored at Collie.*

A 520 class locomotive leaving the station at Belair, South Australia. Twelve engines in this class were built for service during the second World War on the Adelaide-Port Pirie broad-gauge line.

Above: *Ten 700 class Mikado type locomotives were introduced on South Australian Railways in 1926 for freight work. Similar engines were in use on all Australian railways.*
Below: *The 500 class were for many years the largest and most powerful engines in use in Australia. They still hold the distinction of being the most powerful two-cylinder locomotives. Originally constructed as Mountain locomotives for the South Australian Railways, they were converted to a 4—8—4 Northern type*

Above: *One of the few remaining serviceable steam locomotives, the "Duke of Edinburgh" was built at the Islington workshops, South Australia, and placed in service in 1936. Ten of the light Pacific engines were built for passenger services on broad-gauge lines.*

Below: *An S class Pacific type locomotive, streamlined to haul the "Spirit of Progress" from Melbourne to Albury. This class was converted to oil burners in 1951-52.*

Above: *The work horse of Victorian country lines—the N class goods locomotive. Of the fifty-three introduced from 1950, ten were later sold to the South Australian Railways and renamed the 750 class.*

Above: *Locomotive No. 1, built for the Adelaide to Port Adelaide Railway and placed in service in 1855. It was converted to a tender locomotive in 1869 (as shown) and withdrawn two years later.*
Below: *The first locomotive built at Gawler, South Australia—an R class 4-6-0 engine, weighing sixty-four tons*

Above: *Camelmen present a message of loyalty and welcome to the Governor of Western Australia at the official opening of the Coolgardie line on 24 March 1896.*

Below: *A timber train of the 1870s, with a load of sleepers from the forests of south-west Western Australia*

At first she ran from Fremantle to Guildford, but in 1906 was bought by a private timber company and for the next 36 years she helped open up the great karri and jarrah industry for the State. She hauled thousands of logs, visited many bush towns and districts. When she was done with and beyond repair, she was left to rust. In 1956 the Western Australian Government Railways reclaimed her with a full restoration face-lift, and now she holds pride of place in the Department's Railway Exhibition Hall.

The performance of some of these early colonial-built engines was the equal of the great stream-liners of today, all things considered. Take this report of the Melbourne and Hobson's Bay Railway Company one month after the opening of this, the first railway in the land—and still using the locomotives they had made themselves as those ordered from Britain had not arrived.

"*20 October 1854:* Up to Tuesday evening the total number of persons who have travelled over the line since it was opened was 34,207. This is a large return when it is considered that fully two-thirds of the work has been done by the ballast engine, in consequence of the disablement of the large locomotive. The number of persons conveyed during the first seven days was 5,690, while in the week ending October 17th the number was 8,207.

"The Colonial-made engine is again at work, and the curve at the Melbourne end being now avoided—a new road having been made from the northern end of the bridge to the rear of the station—the train starts with the utmost ease.

"The alteration in the line referred to has, of course, been a very expensive affair, and indeed the superiority of the new terminus over the old one is obvious, that it seems singular that Mr Moore, who is high in favour as a competent engineer should not have discovered earlier that the avoidance of an awkward curve was practicable. The trains are now running with great punctuality."

The rusting relics of the steam age—a partly stripped locomotive at a country siding

A Beyer Garratt locomotive, the largest steam locomotive to be placed in service in Queensland (1950). Nineteen were built in England, and eleven in France; each engine weighs 137 tons

THE SHAKERS OF MOUNTAINS

"THEY WERE THE MONARCHS of an age," Ernest Renner, the old driver, recalled. When he retired in 1964 he should have known: he had spent forty-eight and a half years on the footplate. "Those little puffing billies of the old days were all right, I suppose, but in my day we drove the engines that shook mountains. The whole earth trembled to our passing."

Ernest Renner joined the Western Australian Government Railways in April 1914. At first he was a call-boy—riding his bicycle round calling the loco drivers ready for their shifts. "They were supposed to come and sign my book to prove that they had been wakened. Imagine a small, fifteen year old boy insisting on one of these powerful, big men doing anything. I don't think I was ever game enough to wait once I heard them begin to move. There were five call boys in Perth. When our bikes broke down we walked all over the city, from dusk to dawn, calling thirty to forty men." For this he was paid three shillings a day. When he graduated to cleaner at eighteen, he got six shillings a day.

"In those days the top drivers had their own locos and own mates—fireman and cleaner and such. And so the engines were well cared for and woe betide the cleaner who didn't do his work well. The driver had authority to sack the cleaner. But that wasn't necessary. When it was your own regular engine, you took a lot of pride in it, and in your work. That first lot of mates I was with, the fireman used to come to work an hour before his time to polish the brass work of his engine. Drivers used to work in an official uniform, a black shirt and white tie, and us young 'uns secretly longed for the day when we too would wear that gear.

"When I started in cleaning at night the shift boss was a real terror. Instead of giving us all the engines at once, he'd let them down one at a time, so he could keep his eye on us. One of his tricks was to come down to the shed and put a light on one end of the pit to see how many legs he could see dangling down from where we used to catch a wink of sleep. Doing eighteen hours a day, you needed that odd nap, too.

"One night this boss was letting down some coal trucks from the stage and got the top of his thumb caught between two buffers. He was hollering out. After two hours a policeman came along and told us he could hear him hollering up on the coal stage. So someone climbed up and released him. Another night, the crane on the coal stage had its fire bars burnt out, so we went up and took the fire out of it. Up he came to see what we were doing, his great big beard and grey whiskers sticking out and he stuck his head in the fuelbox and—goodbye whiskers. Nobody told him we'd just taken the fire out of the box."

Then it was his turn to take the loco out into traffic. "You'd waited so long and the job had become such a part of you that you took it in your stride. This is how we worked, the routine for a driver before taking his engine out into traffic. Come on, sign on, open the locker for your mate, your fireman. Then look at the notice board, the notice about your train.

"Get your kit out of locker, and fireman gets his. Detonators, red flag, spanners, wool for trimming, gauge glasses, lubricating glasses, corks and any other tools. Each

Above: *The South Coast Daylight, New South Wales Railway, on its scenic run close to the Pacific Ocean.*
Below: *The Central West Express, New South Wales Railways*

Above: *Two Rx locomotives haul the Adelaide to Melbourne express near Belair, South Australia, in the 1920s. These engines gave over fifty years of service to South Australian Railways.*

Below: *Approaching Richmond before electrification—an early publicity photograph of the Victorian Railways*

man has his own personal idiosyncrasies, for instance I took pliers. Oil up your engine, carefully examining bolts, nuts, springs, engine gears to see that there's nothing loose, nothing that might cause an accident on the track.

"Then you blow down your engine. Open your valve and blow the water out; water too soft will undo you. You've got scum cocks to blow scum off the top of the water and blow-off cocks to blow the mud from the bottom of the boiler.

"The fireman gets his kit from the locker, shovel, water bag, pick (for long journeys), his bucket that holds shifting spanner, brush, hammer, lights for gauge glass, waste, and last but most important, the billy for tea.

"The engine cleaner already has the fire on; actually the shed fireman keeps fires going all the time. He has to have forty pounds of steam or over before the engine crew come on. You examine the smoke box, the smoke arrester. If dirty, clean. I tell you, you move. Put on the smoke arrester, clean the slide, steam your engine out to water column to take water in.

"Now you see a sight. There in the morning, with the haze lifting off the frost and the dawn coming up and you and your mates steaming out of the round house, a great flag full of steam rolling round you.

"While we take on water you examine your fire tools: fire shovel, plugging iron, dart (to clean the tube plate), pricker, rake. You carry sand, so you fill the sand boxes. Then you get back into the cab and fill the lubricator and see that all sand gear is working. Sand is a safety device and it's not only used for wheels slipping on rails but if you're having difficulty with your brakes, sand gives more adhesion and stops a slip. Then you take your engine to the coal stage for coal. You've got three-quarters of an hour to do all this.

"Before a driver takes an engine on a trip he must know the road he will be running. You've got to learn your landmarks—house, windmill, certain tree, gravel pit, each set your own individual landmarks. If you're running short of steam, you know the sections where you can shut off your regulator and roll to give the fireman a chance to gain steam again—you can even do this going *up* a hill if you know your road well enough. There are little places where you can shut off.

"A driver had to have three trips over the road with a pilot before he was considered to know the road, before he knew it well enough to make momentum work for him. You wanted to make it smooth going for your engine, didn't want to knock it around. When they brought in the pooling system that ended the days of a driver having his own individual engine. We used to care in those days.

"We took our holidays when our engine went in for annual overhaul. None of this letting anyone push it around like a wheelbarrow, not with these magnificent monsters."

From the viewpoint of the fireman, there was a lot more to his job than just shovelling coal. "I always make my fire go as far as possible," a fireman said. With each State system burning up to $2 million of coal each year, the pressure was always on the fireman and driver to economise.

"No fireman wantonly burns coal. The fireman's job is to always keep a full head

Top left: *North Melbourne coal stage, 1927.*
Top right: *Jack Wilson (right) and mate on the Warragul (Victoria) coal stage, 1918.*
Below: *Over the ash-pits at Tailem Bend, South Australia*

Above: *This elegant parlour car was in service for the Victorian Railways in 1906.*
Facing page: *Double-banking on a turntable at Peterborough, South Australia, in 1910.*
Class T No. 254 at front, and Class K No. 52 at rear

of steam and a full pot of water. You must have the safety valve just on the 'pop.' You get along better and we use less coal, *much* less coal."

All firemen were adamant on one thing. "A man is best able to fire his engine to advantage when he has a regular mate. Knowing your mate's method is important. A man can anticipate and respond to his driver's needs. You've also got to know your road, make preparations as you proceed, anticipate the arrival of banks by building your fire some distance in advance. Never let your fire get too thin. And learn your engine. Always drop the damper when rolling.

"I always get to work well before time to have a quick look over her. I like to have my fire burnt through before starting. Never use the pricker, and keep the damper open with a thick fire."

For economical working, the complete combustion of the fuel in the firebox was necessary. "To do this a fireman must always keep a bright fire. The correct way to build it is heap the coal heavy in both back corners of the firebox, and along both sides and taper towards the tube plate in front. The fire should be lowest in the middle, so that the draught can come through."

And there he'd stand, his blue calico cloth cap over his hair, his overalls loose, and his arms free. And then he'd kick the firebox door open and begin to swing a rhythm a dancer might envy; one to the left rear of the box, turn, thrust, swing and toss, one to the right rear of the box, turn, thrust, spin, and wave one right down the centre, stamp on the footplate and the butterfly doors close down the flare of the fire and the heat of the coals.

"Mind you, there's a lot in working the door and the damper," says the fireman, the black dancer of the footplate.

*   *   *   *

"Jack Wilson and I contracted for the Warragul coal stage after his mate, Bill Martin, chucked it in. Up till then they'd taken me on at times as third man. We contracted to load all the trains from Neerim, Traralgon, Melbourne and the local as well. The contract covered emptying the ash pit and loading the ashes and unloading the wood trucks—the wood used to get the fires going in the engines.

"Up on the landing on the coal stage were five barrows. They held twenty-eight hundredweights of coal. We'd shovel the coal in and fill them up then run them out on rails and tip them into the tender. Sometimes we'd shovel it in if the coal was high enough to save us double handling. We got ten pence a ton for loading the engine. Emptying the ash pit was a cow of a job. We had to shovel it up and out and then load it into trucks. We got seven shillings and six pence a truck for that. We got next to nothing for unloading the wood trucks.

"Loading the barrows up top with coal we'd work two men left handed and right handed to fill up a barrow. One day Jack Wilson brought a mate over to work third man for us. This bloke came straight from the pub. 'Which hand do you use?' Jack said to him. 'I use both hands,' said the bloke. 'For shovelling,' said Jack, 'which hand will you use?' 'If I can't use both me hands, you can keep your bloody job,' said this fellow and heads back to the pub.

"Of course, you didn't get a third man easy, even in those days. Some days Jack Wilson and I started work at seven in the morning and our wives didn't see us until one the next morning. But mostly it was twelve hour shifts. The engine drivers were all good blokes. Get up with a shovel and lend us a hand if time was pinching us or a bad lot of coal. Sometimes when they'd file the docket in our hut, saying how many tons we'd loaded them, they'd add a ton or so.

"Maitland coal we used for passenger trains and Eastern area coal from Wonthaggi for goods. Of course when the Commissioner's train came through, it was Maitland coal and bring out the hose, lads, and water the dust down."

Above and below: *The Sentinel, North Australia Railway, Darwin, Northern Territory. Known locally as "Leaping Lena," this old rail car served for many years*

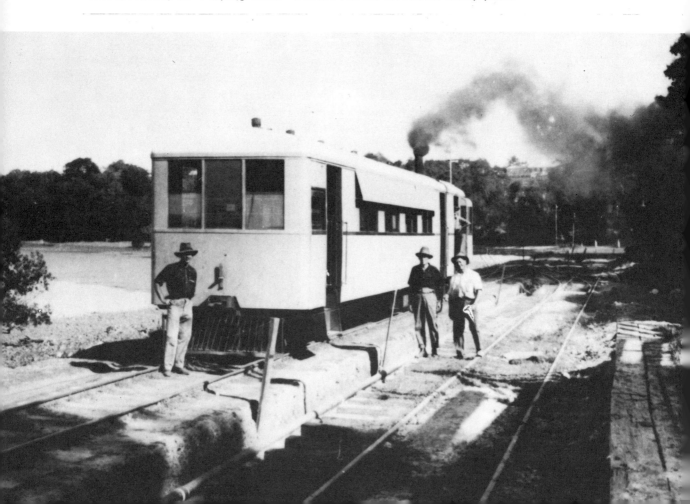

THE LEAPING LENA'S

THE LEAPING LENA no traveller would ever forget was stationed at Darwin. Officially named "The Sentinel" this old smut-blowing ("smut-engendering" the driver used to say) motor was well known to thousands of soldiers in the second World War. They painted their title on her side, "Spirit of Protest," almost a term of endearment rather than indignity.

A description of the railway journey from Port Darwin to Pine Creek on this train was written by Mr T. Southwell Keely. "When an intending passenger reveals that he is making a journey from Darwin down the line 'just for the trip' townspeople gather to see the train pull out of Darwin Station, and, with a series of jolts and jerks, which it maintains with unfailing regularity throughout the journey, so that one braces oneself in readiness for the next shattering jar and is disappointed if it does not occur, the trip to Pine Creek begins. 'Leaping Lena,' as the engine is known all along the route, blows a thin whistle, and shortly afterwards a cloud of steam and coal dust sweeps through the compartment. The train is off!! A dog pursues it, races down the road, overtakes the engine, and, well in the lead, disappears in the scrub ahead. 'Leaping Lena' was maintaining her steady eighteen to twenty miles per hour. Within a few minutes the train enters the scrub which surrounds the town, and the narrow gauge rails stretch out in front through a tapering clearing; not the shining rails of southern lines, but rust encrusted, for the train runs but once a week. The monotony of the Australian bush, mile after mile of the same type of stunted trees and scrub, is maintained to the terminus.

"The overland telegraph line skirts the railway, stretching out through the heart of the continent to link Darwin with Adelaide. Frequently the poles are feet under water and for miles the train will run through a waterlogged country. Shallow rivers and billabongs have overflown and the country has been flooded on either side of the line. The monotonous dull green of the stunted trees is leavened by the more brilliant green of the tall spear grass which fringes the track and grows right up to the rails. Ten and twelve feet it grows, and memories of travelling on a Northern Territory train during the wet or monsoonal period would never be complete without the swishing sound of the grass brushing continuously along the sides of the carriages. Masses of grass pile up beneath the carriages, and their insistent swishing has cut deep into the grain of the running boards. Seas of tall, rank grass billow on either side, making the undergrowth appear dense, impenetrable jungle. In a few months, however, it will wither away beneath the fires and fierce sun of the waterless dry season and expose the hard brown surface soil."

There were "Leaping Lena's" all over the nation. Colin Mackie, a Tasmanian, footloose and wandering in the Depression, knew an odd line. "In the north-west of Western Australia there was a short railway line, quite unconnected with the rest of the State's railways. This line connected the gold-mining town of Marble Bar with Port Hedland, 115 miles away. As the output from the mines at Marble Bar declined so did the importance of the railway, but it still served the sheep stations along the route, bringing in supplies and taking their wool to the port for shipment.

"When I first knew this line, back in 1930, times were hard and even up in the sparsely-settled north-west quite a number of swaggies were on the move. Naturally these people used the railway, but on this particular line nobody expected them to ride in goods trucks; they were made welcome in the passenger compartments. But there was one set rule—if you couldn't pay your fare you were expected to travel second-class."

It was of this "Spinifex Express" that the story was told about the engine driver throwing seeds out on to the side of the track. A passenger hanging out for air had watched him all day as the train crawled over the desert from Port Hedland to Marble Bar. During the afternoon the passenger strolled up to the engine (the story goes that the train didn't have to pull up, or even slow down for that to happen). "What are you doing, mate?" the passenger said to the driver. "Throwing tomato seeds out on the side of the line!" And the engine driver told him why. "The guard's picking tomatoes."

One line in Australia depends to this day on a "Leaping Lena." It's the Normanton to Croydon line in north-western Queensland. Running from nowhere to nowhere now, the line may seem redundant to an onlooker, but to the locals of Normanton the railway and the town still form one of the outposts that used to be titled a "bastion of civilization," according to Stan Tuesley.

Drama or not, if Normanton were to disappear there would be a lot of map with little on it. The dot on the map that signifies Normanton is as important to the nation as was the flag on the end of a pole that the old empire builders used to erect. It is a rallying point for over ten thousand square miles.

The first men came in bullock wagons and camel teams, carting ore from the mines at Cloncurry to the Norman River, where boats took it down to the sea. Soon this traffic was so impressive that the Queensland Government decided to build a railway from Cloncurry to Normanton. Work was started on the earth works in 1888, and twenty-six miles were laid down before work was stopped: Croydon in the east had struck gold. It was decided the line would go that way. The ninety-four mile track was opened in 1891 using iron sleepers to defeat the white ants.

For a little over a decade Croydon and nearby Golden Gate boomed. Three or four trains a week ran to Normanton, where the ore was shipped down the river to the Gulf of Carpentaria. Until the mines began to falter in 1906 these two towns were so buoyant that Normanton expanded on their overflow. To be the port for such mining centres was no small matter. Government offices were set up, customs, local government authorities, and all the facilities such a river port needed. Of course it was different from most Australian places. A railway engineer inspecting the line one year reported that, standing on the rail tracks on the wharf, he watched crocodiles "lazily disporting themselves by the piles." In other ways it was like any port near a mining town in the days when a bonanza meant free spending. On Saturday evenings at six-thirty a train loaded with eight carriages of mining families rolled into Croydon from Golden Gate to shop and parade the streets.

Normanton people with relatives or friends came up and stayed overnight. So many crowded the streets and money flowed so freely in Croydon that when fettler

The Kimberley Express ran between Marble Bar and Port Hedland, Western Australia. The open carriages were no doubt very pleasant in the heat of day

Bill Zahner of Normanton went to Sydney for Christmas in 1911, he came home disappointed. "The streets in Croydon were more crowded on a Saturday night," he complained. "Sydney was quiet by comparison. In Croydon we had to jostle and elbow our way down the street."

Now Golden Gate is deserted and mullock heaps are the only evidence of settlement. Croydon is little better. As the terminal of the line, it boasted a substantial railway station (until 1969 when a cyclone blew it away). It has a hotel and a few shops.

If detractors of railways sneer about the service on this line, the locals don't. They know their numbers and lack of freight (rarely 1,000 tons a year and a passenger list of a few Aborigines only) merits no more than they have got in the old motor train.

But if this is all the traffic, is there any necessity to keep the line open? Jack Rice and Bill Zahner, who were both born at Croydon and worked on the line all their lives, say it is an important line. Jack said, "This town is doomed. It's been doomed since the gold mines failed forty years and more ago. If the railway goes, the place is finished." Would that matter? Bill said, "If this place disappears, there will be a whole great area on the map of Australia without an outpost, without a mark that shows a town exists and with it law and order and all those other things that turn a wilderness into a civilization."

Stan Tuesley, the man that is doing much to keep this outlying flag flying just simply likes the place. "I know it's a joke to a lot of people. They find I'm Officer-in-Charge of a line that's as crooked as a dog's hind leg with the heat and hidden in lush

Above: *Taking "Butch" on board—Normanton to Croydon line, Queensland.*
Below: *Pay day at Normanton Railway Station. Officer-in-charge Stan Tuesley acts as paymaster, driver, station master, accountant, and fitter*

Top left: *Normanton Railway Station, Queensland.*
Top right: *On this 94-mile line, the per-way gang camps out.*
Below: *Another Queensland Railways rail motor, about 1925*

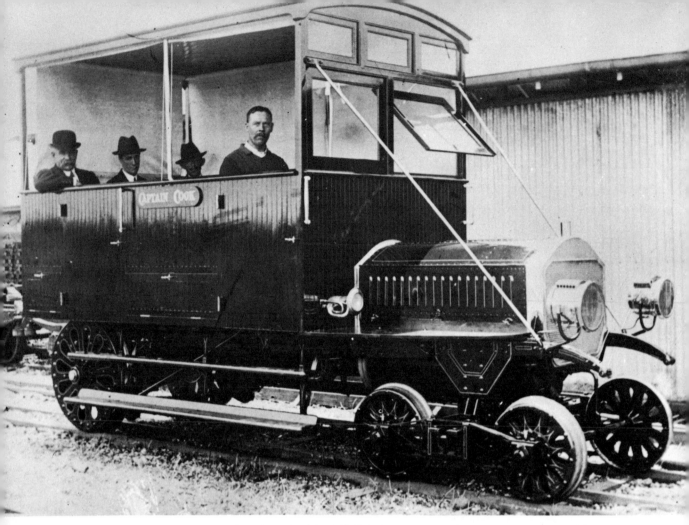

seasons with waist high grass and serving only a couple of hundred people over its
whole length. They don't see anything more than that. And I'm too busy to tell them."
Content, too. Where else could the Officer-in-Charge, driver, paymaster, accountant,
Station Master and qualified fitter pull up his train beside his own house to take on
Butch, his dog, each week on his way to his home station—as well as test his ingenuity
in keeping in running order the oldest stock on the rails in Australia?

There are eight men keeping this line going, four are Thursday Islanders—three
fettlers and the guard, Alfred Callope. Keith McIvor, the ganger, takes his gang out
on Monday morning and camps until Friday night at the lonely sidings. The Station
Master at Croydon sees the Officer-in-Charge-cum-Station Master of Normanton
once a week. This dispersal of their meagre staff doesn't dilute their assurance. When
the Queensland Railways named their modern mainlines after their routes ("Inlander,"
"Sunlander," etc.), the men of the line to the Gulf of Carpentaria rebelled against their
exclusion from this glamour treatment. On a piece of tin fastened to the side of one
of their trucks they painted "Gulflander."

The train runs once a week now, from Normanton to Croydon on Tuesday, and
back to Normanton on Wednesday.

The last of the steam engines was dismantled and the boiler sold to the mines in the

1920s when a "motor" arrived. It came by sea. "We all went down to the wharf to look at it, the whole town," Bill Zahner said. "It was a wonderful new-fangled thing."

The "new-fangled thing" was a Panhard Levassor of 1906 vintage, with chain wheel drive. It was replaced later with a 1920 vintage A.E.C. rail motor similar to the passenger buses on the streets of London at that period. These two old stagers are today the entire motive power of the Normanton line. The report book in the office is full of references to their disabilities. On some occasions they have both been out of service and the run has been made on the fettler's trolley. Even the fettler's trolley was a rare piece of equipment. Its original role as the first rail Ambulance on the Queensland railways is still evident. When the new Casey Jones arrived, Garvie Rice, a fettler and son of a fettler on the line refused to travel on it. "Too fast," he said of the twenty m.p.h. motor. Instead, he rode behind on a trailer it drew which carried drinking water.

For the centenary celebration in August 1968, Stan Tuesley did up the old Panhard and with the A.E.C. was ready for any way the railways might be called on to help with the entertainment. Stan's job makes him a one-man band. The Officer-in-Charge here must be a qualified fitter (Stan completed his apprenticeship in 1926), a manager,

Facing page: *The first passenger rail car in use in Queensland, 1916-1924. Named "Captain Cook," it was a 45 h.p. Napier rail car and served on the Cooktown-Laura line.* Below: *A 153 h.p. Leyland petrol rail car, Queensland Railways, about 1925*

a paymaster for the men he both engages and dismisses, a Station Master at Normanton, and a driver of the train. He's a J.P. and as Resident Officer finds himself on almost all the Boards and Committees of the town. His "museum," as he calls his rolling stock, takes up a lot of his time; repairs are necessary after almost every trip. The three motors—the A.E.C., the Panhard, and the fettler's trolley are rare exhibits and made rarer still by being in constant use.

The Three Cap Pooh-Bah of Cooktown was, like the one-man band of Normanton, a Jack of all trades. On this remote line, the Officer-in-Charge was more than likely to be found in overalls, at work on the things he was in charge of. An indication of the variety of work entailed (or perhaps just an example of having to search through all branches for a suitable man) is given in the records of those men in charge from the opening of the line in 1885 until its closing in 1962. They were drawn from all three railway branches, Traffic, Maintenance, and Locomotive—even though the O.I.C. was in charge of all these three branches of his own line. His salary was paid in a three-pronged allocation of so much for each branch he superintended. He was Station Master, loco driver, and line foreman.

Like most of the lines the other side of the Black Stump, the Cooktown-Laura line was amusing only to the visitor. To the O.I.C. and the people it served, it was just a part of life. It wasn't fenced—there were less than three miles of its sixty-seven miles length taken up by private property, and it ended vaguely at a bridge which it didn't use. For seventy-six years this isolated track stabbed out towards the Palmer River goldfields that, in 1873, had caused the Queensland government concern in finding a route to it from the coast.

Cooktownites would see nothing unusual in the light-railed (forty-one and three-quarter pound) line. In 1888, some years after the earliest route mapping, the surveyors of an extension to the line were still being harried by the Aborigines of that area, who were known for their ferocity. The surveyors reported having been prevented from carrying on their work at times by unfriendly Aborigines.

Cooktown at that time still boasted the tree to which the *Endeavour* was tied when Cook repaired his ship in 1770. From the time of the Captain, few men had rested at Cooktown until the cry of gold brought them. Within a year it was estimated that 41,000 people had converged on the area, and Cooktown developed quickly and had a settlement of 4,000. Before the 1880s began, it boasted sixty-two hotels. Some reports claim there were eighty hotels on the Palmer field itself, in the hinterland from Cooktown. It was declared a municipality, and by the mid-1880s had four newspapers, one of which was printed in Chinese.

The goldfields petered out in a few years—the railway failed to reach the fields— and the miners tore off to another rush and with them went most of the population. Some of the fine buildings remained until recent years although few are intact today; the station and the train remained.

In the early days it was steam, but for its last thirty-four years only small rail motors serviced it once a week. The most famous of these, "Captain Cook," was a Napier motor car, converted in 1916 to rail use. It could carry eleven passengers and the driver(who of course was the O.I.C.), and they were protected from waist up only by canvas blinds. To get her started, the O.I.C. got out the handle and cranked her up, and when the forty-five horsepower under her bonnet responded, the whole five and three quarter foot width of her trembled like a concertina. Later, two trailers were built to be hauled along behind and these carried goods or up to 16 passengers travelling in what, in effect, were open goods trucks with roofs and canvas blinds.

"Captain Cook" coughed away up and down the line where few passengers and as little freight was forthcoming until 1924 when a Studebaker was converted. It was quite presentable, a trustworthy car, but not so well loved by the people of the Cape who remained loyal to "Captain Cook" to the day the line closed.

Later rail-cars had Westinghouse braking equipment, but "Captain Cook" and the Studebaker had no such refinements; they had only mechanical brakes, a toy-like thing when these motors were mounted on rails and the old drivers had many a lively moment on a down-grade. A train "broke" on a trip just after the end of the second World War when they were taking a five ton road truck out to Laura. The driver looked behind to see this wagon with its heavier-than-his-motor load charging down at him from a hill. "What did I do?" he said when he got safely to the end of the line. "I just went faster. What else could I do?"

Wee Georgie Wood, the most famous of all the mountain engines, at Tullah, Tasmania

Above: *A section of the Mount Lyell haulage way, Queenstown, Tasmania, showing the one-in-sixteen incline using the Abt toothed centre rail system*

Above: *The first train on the Marrawah tramline, western Tasmania.*
Centre: *A steam locomotive on the Emu Bay Railway with a load of tin from Mount Bischoff.*
Below: *The main street of Zeehan, Tasmania, as it appeared in 1903. The Emu Bay Railway ran down the main street*

A Beyer Garratt locomotive crossing the Pieman Bridge, Emu Bay Railway, Tasmania

The mountain railways were the real "character lines" of railways. Their very reason for being gave them a personality no other line could have. Built on the small gauge for economy as well as the fact that the terrain allowed no wider track, the railways had the great compensation that the countryside through which they climbed was the most beautiful and unspoiled in the land, a combination that made the journey the most friendly, charming, joyful experience for the odd visitor and the most gratifying work for the railmen.

"When the myrtle was losing its leaf in the gullies and the ground was golden with its fall, the men would pull "Wee Georgie" up and let us get out and pick some for our vases," old Mrs Richardson of Tullah, Tasmania, recalled. Her son, Bert Richardson said, "It seemed a pity to keep all that scenery for ourselves. We liked to share it with the passengers."

All these mountain lines were beloved by the small communities they served and by the men who worked them. The wild and majestic mountains of Tasmania's "wild and woolly West Coast" had the greatest concentration of these lines and an awe-inspiring sight it was to see these Lilliputian beauties going flat out (for them!) round the ridges cut into mountains where men had never lived.

The Fairlies, the Baldwins, and the Dubs, the "giants" of the Lilliputian railways, sizzling quietly as they waited at the stations, would "get under way" when they were opened up and the carriages would swing behind them like a line of conga dancers.

Once criss-crossed with railway lines owned by half a dozen different concerns, the West Coast now has only one line, the Emu Bay Railway, owned by Electrolytic Zinc Company of Australasia Limited. They all seemed to go together. In the 1950s you could travel from Burnie down to Zeehan by Emu Bay Railway; from Zeehan to Strahan by Tasmanian Government; and from Strahan to Queenstown by Mount Lyell Mining and Railway Company Limited. On the way you could stop off at Farrell siding and go into Tullah on "Wee Georgie Wood" of the North Mount Farrell Company. Suddenly, they were gone.

In August 1961, the first road into Tullah was built. The *Advocate* of northwest Tasmania reported: "Isolation of the tiny West Coast mining centre of Tullah came to an end yesterday when the Premier (Mr Reece) cut a ribbon to open the first stage of the new West Coast outlet road. The new nine and a half mile road from Rosebery to Tullah gives access to some of the most spectacular mountain and forest scenery in Tasmania. It is the first road cut to the settlement which has relied for many years on the rail link provided by 'Wee Georgie Wood.'"

Mr Reece said the Tullah mine had worked continuously for about seventy years with the diminutive locomotive, "Wee Georgie Wood," as its only means of communication with the rest of the State. "Sometimes in cases of emergency, this lack of road communication has meant that injured persons have had to be brought out of Tullah by rail under great difficulty. At times it has also meant that doctors and nurses have had to travel to Tullah by rail taking a longer time than should be necessary."

Australian newspapers have never had railway journalists, in the sense of employing journalists who understood railways. In fact some rail fans compile cuttings of the slips made by newspapers today. However, the *Advocate* has, by design or accident, a writer who also knows and loves trains and the running of them in his neck of the woods. Kerry Pink is this man. He wrote a graphic account of the approaching retirement of "Wee Georgie Wood."

"Until the road gangs moved in a couple of years ago, nothing much ever happened at Tullah to break the monotony of life in an inland mining town.

"Consequently, almost every man who was not underground mining silver lead, and every woman and child was at the railway station one day in 1924—no one remembers the exact date—to watch the arrival of the new locomotive that would provide their sole transport to the world outside their small town in the mountain.

"And for those miners not particularly interested in locomotives, the hotel was conveniently opposite the station. It still is.

"The new loco that was driven proudly into Tullah that day was not big—a mere Shetland pony in the family of iron-horses. It was built to suit the light two foot gauge line it was to travel. Nor was it built for speed. It was never intended to travel at much more than six miles an hour and it seldom has.

"But it was fresh from the workshops of Fowler Bros., London, and it shone with the black lustre of a well polished wood stove. And as they inspected their brand new iron-pony, the miners of Tullah saw a shiny brass plate on which was inscribed a name unfamiliar to most of them—'Wee Georgie Wood.'

"This was the stage name of a popular English comedian of the time and the men of Fowler Brothers had evidently considered 'Wee Georgie Wood' an appropriate name for the rather comical little locomotive they had built to serve the mine and miners of Tullah, Tasmania. And so the tiny engine of iron and steel was given a personality, and from that day to this the people of Tullah have referred to 'Wee Georgie Wood' as 'he' and not 'it.' He has become very much one of the town.

"Probably Wee Georgie Wood, the comedian, went out of business a long time ago. 'Wee Georgie Wood,' the locomotive didn't. After thirty-seven years of almost constant toil, 'Wee Georgie' is still slowly but determinedly hauling his freight and passengers over the six miles between Tullah and Farrell siding on the Emu Bay Railway, six days a week.

"But the little loco, which has become known throughout Australia by magazine articles, photographs, and the tales of tourists, is nearing the end of the line.

"The Tullah-Rosebery road, officially opened yesterday by the Premier (Mr Reece) will mean that 'Wee Georgie' has at long last reached retirement. When the road consolidates after a couple of months, the Farrell Mining Company will transport its silver and lead concentrates to Rosebery by road to connect with the E.B.R., and the Tullah-Farrell siding line will be closed.

"What then will be the fate of 'Wee Georgie?' Will he be sold for scrap or continue his labours somewhere else?

"It seems almost certain that the old-fashioned loco, despite purchase offers from several parts of Australia, will remain in his home town. Miners usually are not sentimentalists, but the miners of Tullah are loath to part with 'Wee Georgie.'

"'Our idea is to mount "Wee Georgie" on a cement platform near the new road,' says mine manager, Mr Ron Midson. 'We could sell him, but no one wants us to. It

Above: *Part of the Abt section of the Mount Lyell Railway, Tasmania. The centre rail with its double-toothed cogs enabled the driver to maintain complete control during ascent and descent.*
Below: *Sand drifts on the line from Zeehan to Strahan, Tasmania. The track was relocated three times and eventually abandoned.*

A private line ran from Queenstown to Kellys Basin, Tasmania, in short-lived opposition to the line to Strahan

just wouldn't seem right for 'Wee Georgie' to be anywhere else than right here in Tullah. So we intend to keep him here as a monument to . . . well, to 'Wee Georgie,' I suppose.'

"In his thirty-seven years at Tullah, making two trips a day until recently, 'Wee Georgie' has conservatively made more than 20,000 twelve mile return journeys between the town and Farrell siding.

"Although no express train, he has quite often jumped the line. Sometimes he has rolled down embankments, but with ropes, pulleys and winches, he has been hauled back and repaired. No one remembers anyone ever being seriously injured in any of 'Wee Georgie's' mishaps, although the various drivers over the years have often jumped clear by the skin of their teeth.

"His outward cargo has consisted mainly of silver and lead concentrates—about sixty tons a fortnight in recent years, but more in the boom days—which are taken to Burnie and then shipped to the U.S.A.

"His inward cargoes have consisted of almost everything that has come into Tullah since 1924—food, clothing, school books, beer, explosives, canaries—the lot.

"Probably 'Wee Georgie's' hardest work has been during the past couple of years carrying in machinery and bridge materials for the road that is to bring about his retirement. Some said it would be impossible for 'Wee Georgie' to take the seventy-five foot steel girders for the Murchison River bridge to Tullah, but he did. ' 'Wee Georgie' proved most reliable,' says the P.W.D. District Engineer for the North West (Mr L. J. Bailey).

"And 'Wee Georgie' knows pretty well the history of Tullah's 160 or so residents. He brought most of them into town, and quite a few others who gave Tullah the once-over and left again next day. He has taken young brides into Tullah and then out again later to have their babies. They always leave well in advance, because a ride in 'Wee Georgie' is not recommended for women close to confinement. And he has brought them home with their babies. More than once in his thirty-seven years he has gone through the same routine with the second generation.

"Not many tourists have travelled in 'Wee Georgie,' because most of the people who have visited Tullah in the past have been on business. There isn't really much point in going there, unless it's just to ride the tiny loco. Nevertheless, 'Wee Georgie's' passengers have included a wide variety of people—miners, preachers, politicians, writers, engineers, football teams, housewives, students, and police constables.

"Because it is particularly law-abiding for a mining town, Tullah has no constable of its own. In the past the town has been visited periodically by constables from Rosebery. On occasions when the driver has considered it desirable for the residents to know of the constable's arrival, 'Wee Georgie' has given a pre-arranged signal as he steamed into town.

"'Wee Georgie' has seen quite a few changes at Tullah during his term of residence. The town was well established long before he arrived. Way back in 1892 a lone prospector, T. Farrell, reported the discovery of galena (silver lead) in the area and the ore-bearing mountain was later named after him.

"The North Mount Farrell Company was formed in 1899 on a paid-up capital of

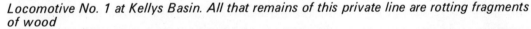

Locomotive No. 1 at Kellys Basin. All that remains of this private line are rotting fragments of wood

£14,000, and the lode has been worked ever since. In the first few years of mining, the ore was taken out by packhorses, but a wooden tramway was built in 1902. This was converted to steam in 1907 when 'Wee Georgie's' predecessor arrived.

"The Farrell mine, like most mines, has had its ups and downs. In its heyday the town had a population of more than 500, but its future looked black in the early 1930s. The ore lode was giving out and the directors announced that the mine would close down. 'No mine, no Tullah,' thought the locals. Just another ghost town. According to the old hands among the Tullahites, the local volunteer fire brigade worked overtime for a few days after the fateful announcement.

"As it turned out, the would-be insurance claimants needn't have worried. About two days before the scheduled shutdown, a group of local diehard miners found a continuation of the lode about half-a-mile north and the present mine is still working this lode.

"Self-professed experts have predicted from time to time that Tullah is on its last legs. Evidently the Government experts don't think so, or they wouldn't have built the costly outlet road to a dying town. 'The shaft is now down about 900 feet and there is no indication of the ore petering out,' says Mr Midson. 'Naturally any working mine is dying all the time. It's not like a farm, where you can put back in what you take out. But the end of Tullah certainly isn't in sight yet.'

"These days motor transport is providing stiff competition for railways, both in private and commercial use. Not so with 'Wee Georgie Wood.' During his life he has reigned supreme, unchallenged, in transport to and from Tullah. Until 1955 the only motor vehicle in Tullah was the company's truck which was used over the half mile between the mine and the town.

"No one in the town had a car, simply because there was nowhere to drive it. But gradually trucks and Land Rovers have been brought into Tullah per 'Wee Georgie,' by the P.W.D. and H.E.C. Now there are also about half a dozen privately-owned vehicles and there will eventually be more, although a group of Hobart car salesmen who went to Tullah last week found the locals were no push-overs for a sale.

"But the advent of road transport should not unduly worry 'Wee Georgie' in his years of retirement. Is it likely that any of these fast, new trucks and cars will serve Tullah as faithfully and as well—or for as long—as 'Wee Georgie Wood?' We think not."

In 1963 Kerry Pink recorded the end of the line for another famous West Coaster. "It was in March 1897 that Queenstown celebrated the official opening of the Mount Lyell Mining & Railway Company at a cost of £216,000 to connect its mines at Queenstown with the port of Strahan. Bowes Kelly, one of the original directors of what is now the Mount Lyell Mining and Railway Co. Ltd, organised the celebrations on a grand scale.

"The Governor (Lord Gormanston) was to have been there, but he didn't make it. The s.s. *Australia* bringing Lord Gormanston and other V.I.P. guests from Hobart to Strahan encountered mountainous seas off Port Davey and had to turn back. The Governor was dreadfully seasick, and when the *Australia* arrived back at Hobart, he was barely able to stagger ashore. When it set out again a day or two later, Lord

Above: *A Dubs locomotive with snow-moving equipment at Guildford, Tasmania, on the Emu Bay Railway.*
Below: *The sand drifts on the West Coast of Tasmania provided great obstacles to the building of railways to connect the hinterland with the coast*

Gormanston was not aboard. But most other invited guests, including a contingent from Melbourne aboard the s.s. *Grafton*, were there for the opening celebrations.

"The Queenstown station was packed with miners and their families as the sturdy little Abt engine named 'Mount Lyell No. 1,' brand spanking new, pulled in with its V.I.P. passengers. On the front of the engine was a copper shield inscribed: *'Labor Omnia Vincit*—We Find a Way or Make It' [literally 'Work Conquers All Things']. And, indeed, the engineers and navvies who built the Mount Lyell railway had done just that.

"The band played, the crowds cheered, flags were waved, and appropriate speeches were made. At night waiters brought from Melbourne served French dishes to the official guests at the Palace Hotel, Strahan, while Herr Holm's orchestra from Zeehan played in the background. All this happened sixty-six years ago.

"On Saturday there were similar scenes at the Queenstown railway station and at Strahan. They were brought about, however, by circumstances quite the opposite of those of 1897. This time Queenstown and Strahan farewelled the now famous railway they had welcomed more than half a century ago.

"It was the same sturdy little Abt locomotive—the first of the five bought for the railway. Its brass plate—'Mount Lyell No. 1'—and the name of its makers, 'Dubs and Co., Glasgow Locomotive Works, 1896' had been polished till they gleamed. A replica of the copper shield and its Latin inscription was there, and below it a wreath from the Locomotive Fitters. On its side was a placard—'Born 1896, Still Going Strong.'

"Almost everyone in Queenstown who owns a camera and many more who don't were there to watch it steam out with its last load of passengers. Unlike the passenger contingent in 1897, these were not what you might call Very Important People. But they were so far as the Mount Lyell railway is concerned. They were the men—some of them well up in their seventies—who have worked on the railway over the years. They came from all parts of the State to make the last passenger trip over the twenty-one miles between Queenstown and Strahan.

"And as the train pulled out from the crowded station, the Queenstown Silver Band played 'Now is the Hour' (the Maori's Farewell), and driver Mick Tatnell sounded the shrill steam whistle of Mount Lyell No. 1—a sound that is familiar to the ears of nearly every man, woman, and child in Queenstown. As the train rattled through South Queenstown, families stood at their doors to wave it farewell.

"When it reached the top of the one-in-sixteen Abt system a few miles out of town—the steepest section of railway in Australasia—it was greeted by more than thirty camera-clicking members of Australian Railways Exploration Association who had come from Melbourne and Sydney especially to see and record this historic trip. They weren't able to travel on the train, so they walked through the bush from the Strahan Road to meet it at Rinadena, the siding at the top of the Abt.

"As the train steamed on—down the other side of the Abt to Dubbilbarril Siding, along the scenically spectacular King River Gorge, over the 900-foot-long King River bridge and into the old river port of Teepookana—the men swapped yarns about the early days and the railway characters who helped create the traditions of the West

Above: *The Commonwealth Railway's "Coffee Pot" ran from Port Augusta to Quorn, South Australia. It is now preserved in the station yard at Alice Springs, Northern Territory.*

Below: *Final run in 1963 for the Abt locomotive on the Mount Lyell Railway, Tasmania*

Coast. They sang a few songs, and their music was provided by the rare combination of bagpipes (piper Lincoln Ladlee) and cornet (bandsman Wally Spooner).

"At Lowana, the last siding before Strahan, there was an unscheduled stop while many of the old hands aboard climbed out to greet—and farewell—their friend, Mrs R. V. Williams. She is a widow of a one-time railway worker and is a friend of almost everyone who has worked on the Mount Lyell railway. There were tears in her eyes—and even some of the old hands were misty-eyed—as they sang 'Auld Lang Syne' and waved their last farewell to 'Mother Williams,' the little old lady of Lowana.

"There weren't many people on the station when the train pulled into the station at Regatta Point, Strahan. One of the locals told me why. 'This is a sorry day for Strahan,' he said, 'and we don't feel like celebrating. And if it comes to that, we don't feel like saying goodbye yet, either. Down here we're all hoping the Government will do the right thing and announce that the line will be kept open for passenger traffic.'

"But there were a few people there, including the local District Nursing Centre sister, who drove the ambulance to the station. Someone remarked that this showed great foresight on the sister's part in view of the big shindig the train's passengers had had in Queenie the night before. However, it turned out that the sister's presence at the station was not solely concerned with the arrival of the train.

"The s.s. *Koonya* was berthed right opposite the station, and Captain Dennis Lambton had hoisted a flag signal which read: 'A Pleasant Journey on Your Departure from Strahan.' The s.s. *Kumalla* was leaving Strahan as the train arrived and her siren sounded a farewell as she glided past. Mick Tatnell did likewise.

"Within seconds of disembarkation at Strahan, all but two or three of the train's 100 or more passengers had disappeared from view. The Hotel Gordon is only a few convenient steps from the station.

"When the train eventually pulled out of Strahan on the homeward journey, I stood beside an old chap who had come to see her off. I don't know who he was or what he was, but he was obviously not the kind given to making profound statements. But as the last of the aged carriages disappeared round the bend, he said, more to himself than to me, 'Well, that's the end of an era.' And indeed it is."

A "rack rail," similar to that used on part of the Queenstown to Strahan line, was also used on the Mount Morgan line in Queensland. The third, or centre rail, was toothed. This enabled the train to haul itself up—or ease itself down—a steep grade.

This aid to alpine engines was patented by Dr Roman Abt in Switzerland in 1882. The stepped track is a double bar, the teeth on one opposite the gaps on the other. The locomotive is fitted with a double pinion, also stepped to engage with the stepped or toothed track, giving a continuous firm engagement.

Even with this aid the mountain trains were difficult to control coming down the one in sixteen grades. "Did she ever get away on you?" George White, guard-brakesman on the Mount Lyell was once asked. "No," he said. "But I've had some bloody fast rides."

In a section all their own, quite apart from any other railway, were the timber lines.

A load of giant logs being hauled to the mill at North Dardanup, Western Australia

At various times in the past, their tracks have covered nearly as many miles as the official railways themselves, and for ingenuity they most certainly would top all. Western Australia, Tasmania, New South Wales, and Queensland all had their timber lines, but the most active certainly were in Western Australia. The records of Western Australian Government Railways are quite repetitious when reporting on the fate of outdated governmental expresses, "Sold to timber firm."

May Vivienne on her walkabout in 1882 travelled in the big timber country, and on the tracks of the "little wonders." Down near "The Valley of the Giants" she noted: "Seven miles farther on are Millar's Yarloop Mills. The export from these mills is very large; twenty-one sailing ships and fifteen steamers were employed to take away the timber to various places last year. The settlement presents a busy appearance. When the train stopped, over 100 men came from the mills to get their newspapers and see if there was anyone they knew in the train. I left the train and looked for an hotel to put up at, but there is none; however, I obtained comfortable quarters at a private house.

"There are several mills connected with Yarloop, among them Iron Pot, so called from a conical hill near to it. Hoffman & Waterhouse's Mills are thirteen miles away, and are connected by telephone with the head mill. The office is very handsomely built of jarrah lined with polished wood, tongued and grooved. No liquor is allowed to be sold at the mill on account of the dangerous nature of the occupation, consequently this is a model township. There are several coffee-houses, and, in spite of their enforced sobriety, the men seem to be very jolly and happy. An enormous stack of timber was ready to be shipped to Colombo, and the men were at work cutting more, as the enormous demand for Western Australia wood keeps the workmen busy night and day, working in relays.

"The train line wound round the hills in picturesque fashion, until we came to a valley which looked more picturesque still, but rather dangerous to cross in a timber-train. Here the flying fox or aerial tram is used to bridge the steep part and to carry small timber. I was glad I did not venture down into the valley, for I was afterwards told that it was not an infrequent occurrence for the timber-trucks, and occasionally the engine also, to leave the line, and as the trucks are of the roughest description, consisting merely of four wheels and a platform, and are loaded with immense logs, the passenger can only travel on the engine, or on the 'dummy,' which is a special truck placed immediately behind the engine to keep it from being damaged in case some huge log, weighing perhaps twenty tons, should slide forward in the course of a descent. It is difficult to give an idea of the size of the gigantic Karri trees here. One which I saw was quite hollow, and a bullock team drove right through it with perfect ease. In returning to the town, I saw another large quantity of battens or pickets waiting to be shipped for London to fence two large cemeteries.

"When felled, the tree is marked off into certain lengths and severed into so many logs, then numbers of horses and bullocks appear on the scene and dray the logs to the nearest landing, then they are put into the truck and borne off to the mill. At Baranup, I was to see the King Karri that I had heard about before coming, and now, when I saw it, I was satisfied that, although not yet 400 feet high, it is a king of the forest; indeed, this giant tree is the largest on indisputable record in Western Australia. It stands in its great majesty in one of the most picturesque spots of the Colony. Its gnarled and weather-beaten roots of immense size show that it must be of great age. Its dimensions were given to me by Mr Davies, and are as follows: Girth 4 ft above ground, 30 ft 8 in; Girth 6 ft 2 in above ground, 28 ft 1 in; Girth 132 ft 6 in above ground, 20 ft 7 in; Height to top of branches, 342 ft 0 in; Height to first fork, 146 ft 0 in.

"This tree would make 146 loads of timber and cut up into 3,000 sleepers, enough to lay a mile and a half of railway. Around here are many more tremendous giant trees awaiting the woodman's axe. The demand for Western Australia hardwood is now far greater than the mills can at present supply."

The Western Australian timber railways were three foot six inches gauge, and had far better "permanent way" construction and larger rolling stock and locomotives than those of other States. Millar's Denmark Railway alone was as strong and efficient as many a conventional railway.

At first, Millar's set up mills to cut sleepers for other railway schemes and brought 200 navvies from Victoria for the job in 1889. Eventually they built twenty-eight miles of railway, used not only as a timber track but also for a passenger service twice daily from Denmark to Albany using Philadelphia (U.S.A.) Baldwin 2–4–2 locomotives. These locos were most popular in Tasmania as well.

Some of the engines used on these early timber lines have travelled far from their home lines. Sitting rusted, under a tree in Forrest, Victoria, is the "Tom Cue." As its name suggests, it was originally a native of Western Australia and ran on the Murchison line to Cue. It was named in honour of Tom Cue, the famous prospector of the West. It went first to Tasmania, and after a few years there was bought for Victoria.

An early shunting D.I.E. engine on a timber line in southern Tasmania

The Elizabeth Street entrance to the Flinders Street Railway Station, Melbourne, in the 1870s

STATION STREET

STATION STREET is as much a part of our history as is Main Street or Civic Square. It is not only a place, but a way of life. It was once a stamping ground of the men who made up the "great family of railway workers" as Commissioner Harold (later Sir Harold) Clapp called them. Here was the symbol of the greatest industry of the nation, the loco drivers, guards, fettlers, station masters, and their families who "lived" railways. To them, the railway was not just a way of life, it *was* life.

Dorrie Asquith, now an elderly lady living at Euroa, Victoria, had a typical railway childhood. "I have lots of half forgotten memories of life spent as a child and teenager in railway houses, always such dull brown places, all alike and never any conveniences to lighten the housewives' lot. But as children we were always happy and greeted any new transfer with delighted anticipation.

"My earliest memories are of life at Arcadia on the Goulburn. I was only about three years old and my sister a little older. We were close then to my birth-place, Yarroweyah. My father received notice of transfer to Nowingi in the Mallee. It was promotion but what a terrible wrench to leave a town where he was happy with good mates and could go down to the river any evening and fill a bag with Murray Cod and bream in no time, not to mention the wild duck that were plentiful, and to have to go to a place that was the end of nowhere!

"But the railways have been built up by men like my father who gave forty years of his life to them. He was loyal and conscientious and I can picture him now sitting in the tin shed freezing in winter and boiling in summer writing that innumerable correspondence, often in his own time. It was a nightmare journey, my parents, a young teenage orphaned aunt, my sister and I. There was no station at Nowingi; a step ladder was put into use for us to alight. It seemed all hot burning sand, tea-tree, galvanized iron and goats; and the terrible sore eyes we got.

"When my mother was about to have a third child, the railways gave us a compassionate transfer to Woolamai and my sister was born at Wonthaggi. Oh what utter bliss it must have been for all of us to reach Gippsland. We children were in our glory, exploring those beautiful fern gullies with climbing clematis and the hills carpeted with the glorious pink, red, and white heath. There must have been times when it was wet, cold and muddy but I never remember any of those drawbacks.

"The railways must have been the only means of transport in those times; it was during the first World War. The fishermen used to come to the station with their catches to forward them to Melbourne market and I can remember them giving my father lovely fresh fish and a *bucket* of oysters. Do you know I have never tasted oysters since but I can still taste that delicious tang as sprinkled with vinegar they slid down my throat.

"Our next transfer was to Glenrowan in the north-east. The war was nearing its end; I was due to start school and my mother was to have another child. This one, a boy, was born in Wangaratta. We thoroughly enjoyed our stay in Glenrowan. It was a clean, friendly little town, famous because it was the homeplace of the Kelly Gang. A favourite pastime of we children, frowned upon by our parents, was to wait

EXTRACT FROM RAILWAY ACT. 1863.

THROWING STONES AT RAILWAY TRAIN A FELONY.

XLV. *If any person wilfully and maliciously cast, throw, or cause to fall or strike against, into or upon any Engine, Tender, Carriage, or Truck, used upon any Railway, any wood, stone, or other article, matter, or thing with intent to endanger the safety of any person being in or upon such Engine, Tender, Carriage, or Truck every such person shall be guilty of felony*

XLVI. *Every person convicted of a felony under this Act shall be liable to be sentenced to* IMPRISONMENT WITH HARD LABOR *for any term not exceeding* TEN YEARS.

R.C.
W.I.A

BOARD OF LAND AND WORKS
(Railway Construction Branch)

WANTED
SLEEPERS

Grey Box, Red Ironbark, Red Gum, Red or Yellow Box Timber

Rectangular Sleepers 8ft. 6ins. x 9ins. x 4½ins. price 5/- each on Trucks

Round-top Sleepers   8ft. 6ins. x 9ins. x 4½ins.   „ 4/3 „ „ „

Tender Forms and Specification obtainable from Station Master or from

Plant Officer, Room 88, Railway Offices, Spencer Street, Melbourne

VICTORIAN RAILWAYS.

BOARD OF LAND & WORKS

(Railway Construction Branch).

Employes must not Camp within Fifty (50) Yards of any Running or Still Water which is likely to be required for Human Consumption, and must not Bathe in it or do anything which will cause its pollution.

By Order,

_____

_____18____   6517.7.13

_____

Officer in Charge.

beside the station and as the evening train was pulling out, we would call out lustily "Paaaper Paaaper" and literally pounce on the *Herald* or whatever paper was thrown to us. The highlight for us, of course, was the annual holiday with the free pass. I think Dad always got it about October. Oh, what preparations were made for this.

"Once again my mother went to Wangaratta and brought us home a baby brother and this was the last of our family. Several months after Dad received notice of a transfer to Euroa. Previous to this he had been offered a job as road foreman but it would have meant travelling a lot and he was a real home body and did not accept.

"Once again we packed our belongings. The cow was taken to the station to go in a cattle truck, our faithful dog to the guards' van. The men stacked our furniture in a truck and away it went, presumably to arrive and be ready to meet us, but this plan miscarried. We children went up to catch the late afternoon train loaded up with all our bits and pieces. I was the custodian of our cockatoo. He was nailed down in a wooden box, but nothing daunted Cocky. His beak and claws worked overtime and about halfway through the journey, a bright alert head popped through a hole and with a bright beady little black eye surveying us all, Cocky raised his crest and invited one and all to 'Scratch Cocky.'

"We must have presented a queer spectacle as we left the station, Dad loaded down with the inevitable trunks, Mother with the baby, myself with a wildly excited Cocky wriggling more and more of his body out of the box, my brother leading the dog. We made our way to our new home only to find our furniture had not arrived, electricity was not connected. My father tried unsuccessfully to find a bed for us at the hotels or boarding houses but apparently families were not welcome. So we spent the night on the bare boards covered by a couple of rugs a sympathetic old lady loaned us. My mother received a very severe chill which took months to shake off.

"My parents were to spend a number of years in this railway house, almost until my father's retirement. We all grew up there. We had a very nice garden but the old house was riddled with white ants. I can remember the great fuss when the commissioners were coming on inspection. We tried to make the best of everything and I think living through the great depression cowed many of us and our parents. Even after he retired my father retained his great interest in everything connected with the railways. He had given the best years of his life to it ungrudgingly."

The residents of Railway Row had their own special "monickers," their own lingo, and their own heroes. There was pride, uniquely theirs in an era when jobs were short of "being permanent." Mrs Asquith also recalled: "My husband hadn't had work for five years, and our second child was on the way. He applied for the railways and was called up for the exam. We waited for the result. We were that anxious! Then it came. He wasn't well enough educated. And it was a pick and shovel job he'd sat for!

"So it was correspondence school from the Institute for a year, me giving him spelling and dictation at night. We couldn't afford the daily paper, so it was the Book of Common Prayer, all we had. Rabbiting in the hills all day and when he went to night class, I'd skin them and peg the skins out on the wire frames and next day when he went out again, I'd try to sell fresh rabbits round the town and get home in time to give him his dictation and spelling. His father had died when he was nine and there weren't pensions and things in those days and he was the eldest of six so he'd had to work. Then he sat for the exam again. We hardly talked while we waited for the letter. Then it came. He could start right away in a gang. "We're made!" he shouted at me. And, we were, too."

There are few towns in Australia that have not at one time or another had a Station Street or its equivalent. In suburbs of the cities it might hold "the heads:" the super-intendents, engineers, traffic inspectors, and paymasters. But it was in the country, where it was the crossroads of the community, that its true elan showed. Here lived the Station Master and the fettler, those two footloose men whose wanderlust took them from one station to another. They took with them their skill and experience and the new ideas they picked up on their journeying. It was this injection of new ideas that was the most valuable contribution made to the developing Australian community in isolated outposts. How often did Australians see the local Station Master "in the box" at the annual Ball while the ganger "took the tickets" and their wives "did the supper." There was the annual Race Meeting with the fettling gang repairing the fence and rebuilding the judges' stand (with tea-tree or gum boughs).

The Temperance pledge as presented to employees of the Victorian Railways in the 1890s

Often the only organised, disciplined group of men in an isolated area, they were called to fires, floods, and disaster.

Station Street, or Railway Place, whatever it was called, housed the pillars of bush society. Backing their status was the tight link of the iron rail, the roar of the engine from far-off places as a reminder of another world outside their own insular little nut-shell, the whistle that told of their connection to outside help, the bringing of news, food, mail, and friends.

It was little wonder that the station became a social centre. Settlers came in not only to meet or farewell a friend but "just to see the train come in." In a diary written in Queensland early this century, Roy Medew tells of reaching Theodore, having travelled nearly fourteen hours from Rockhampton, and having to "push my way through the settlers waiting to see the train come in." The railway features in almost all the early diaries.

At Yalgoo, in Western Australia, the station held, literally, the whole population of the town when the train came in. When May Vivienne, a traveller, went there in 1882 she found the town deserted. "Not a soul was about the hotel or the street. I felt like a sailor in a desert." She went into the empty hotel, the Emerald, and sat down, watching two emus stalking about outside the window. "Presently a cook turned up, strange to say, a woman cook, as most cooks in these parts are Japanese men. I asked her for some dinner; she said she had none in the hotel, it was all at the railway station . . . the proprietor of the hotel also caters for the railway station, and his staff goes down there to attend to the train passengers at the dinner hour; everybody who requires dinner being supposed to get it there. The whole male population of Yalgoo goes down to see the train come in; it is the event of the day."

She next set off for Mount Magnet. "On the day I left it was raining heavily, and I had to wait an hour at the station for the train, which was late in arriving. This brought to my mind the story of the gentleman who had promised to attend at a certain place and make a speech, but found himself unable to do so on account of the heavy rains having destroyed a section of the railway line. Accordingly he wired, 'Cannot come; wash out on the line.' The reply came: 'Come anyway; borrow a shirt.'

"At last the train made its appearance, and I took my seat and went to Mount Magnet (not to be confused with Mount Margaret, which is in quite a different part of the country about thirty-two miles farther on.) On arrival there the railway station was so crowded that I could scarcely get out. There were about 300 young men of all sorts and sizes, and with such jolly smiling faces that I began to feel quite hilarious myself. They turned out to be the successful footballers just returned from a match at Cue. Several buggies and horses were waiting at the station, and I had no difficulty in being conveyed to a hotel, which bore the significant name of 'The Oasis.'"

The young nation was having an unsophisticated love affair, more a thing of deep affection. When on 1 July 1892 the South Australian dog named "Bob" turned up in Victoria he merited a column in the railways gazette. "There was a distinguished visitor, and one which attracted marked attention, at the Ararat railway station in

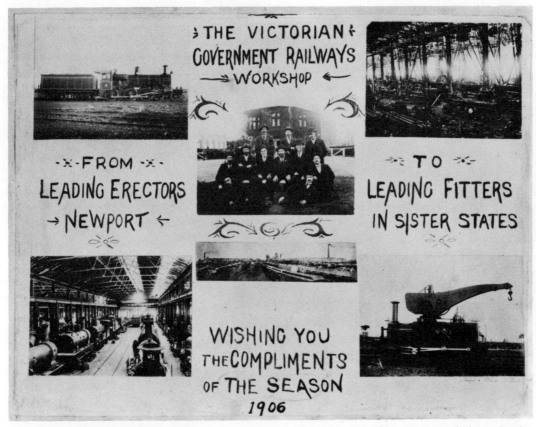

This Christmas greeting of 1906 shows the part played by the Newport workshops in the Victorian Railways system

the shape of 'Bob, the railway dog.' Amongst railway men Bob is, perhaps, the best known free pass traveller on the colonial lines, and he is welcomed at all stations where his predilection for travelling takes him.

"Bob is of the Russian retriever breed, a remarkable looking shaggy black dog, and he has on his neck a collar with a brass plate and his registration number, etc., whilst on the plate the following doggerel is inscribed, 'Stop me not, but let me jog, for I am Bob the driver's dog.' The animal's coat is streaked with grey, for he is in advanced years. His master, who was engaged on the South Australian lines, was killed in a collision, or, in railway parlance, a 'pitch in,' some fifteen years ago. His canine friend escaped and having grown accustomed to life on a tender, he still stuck to the trains, and though petted by all railway men, he remains true to the memory of his first master and attaches himself to no one in particular. Though aged, Bob is a very lively and sagacious animal."

Above: *Latrobe station, Tasmania, during the loading of a "spuds" train*
Below: *N class locomotive No. 252 during the loading of the 1901 wheat harvest at Rupanyup in the Victorian Wimmera district*

Above: *The Sydney Railway Terminus in September 1880. Sailors turned miners are being farewelled by shipmates from the Zealandia as they leave for the Temora diggings.*
Below: *Unloading the wheat train at the Port Pirie wharf, South Australia*

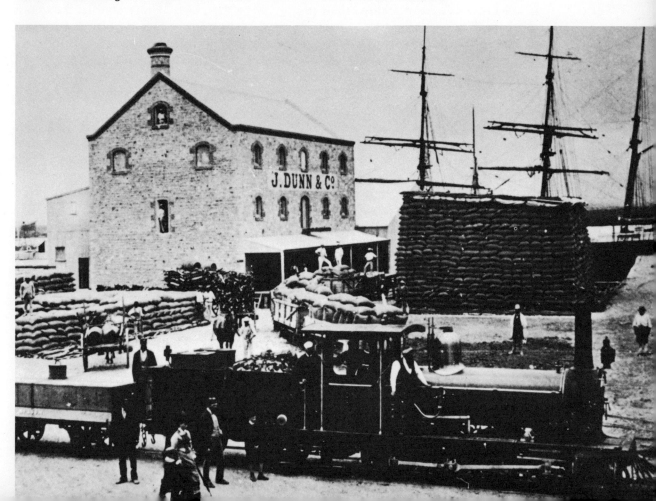

This was for the people The Railway Age: the age when little boys dreamed of becoming engine drivers and their bigger brothers boasted they could "wield a pick and shovel with the best of them." It was a golden age, too, for women. Before it was socially acceptable for women to "go out to work," and the only work offering in the country was domestic drudgery, the wives of railmen had the opportunity to do responsible, interesting work as caretakers (in charge of a small station that had no other staff), or gatekeeper on a level crossing.

From the railway yard came the hum of engines and the clank of couplings and the rumbling of rolling wheels; sounds as restful to those who lived with them as a requiem to the dead out on the hill and a lullaby to the babies in their bassinets.

From Station Street, the long crying wail of the whistle came through the dark stillness of night when settlers were tucked in their beds and made their security seem commonplace, dull, and uneventful. It made the lad decide to leave home, the husband to gaze longingly at the square of window as the one-eyed shaker of mountains rumbled by, lighting up his life for that one brief moment, talking to him in the eerie silence.

Station Street was all these things. It was the pulse beat of a young land.

For some places, particularly the desert areas, the rail went first, and people followed. The Mallee country of Victoria is perhaps the best example of this in Australia. There the rail tracks went first, and settlement followed.

In the booklet they put out to announce their "Back To Underbool" celebrations in 1963, the citizens described their region and settlement. "Cultivated land extends southwards some ten miles to the sand ridges of the desert . . . and northwards some twelve to sixteen miles again to the desert. Settlement moved with the building of the railway, begun in 1909 and officially opened for traffic on 25 June 1912. Prior to this, passengers and goods were carried on the works train.

"The first settler in the Underbool district was Mr Frederick Malkin. He carried his swag out from Ouyen on his first visit, a distance of thirty-one miles. In February, he, with his son, took up permanent residence. At that time the railway line was under construction and the township consisted of a few tents. Mr Malkin grew a small crop of wheat that first year, 1911. Just as settlement moved with the building of the railway line, so, too, did enterprising business-men. The first store-keeper, J. F. Cotter, arrived in 1911 and set up his business in a tent in the railway yard. Fresh bread, meat, and other supplies came out from Ouyen on the construction train.

"When young Dick Foley opened up in business, he used to get bread, meat, and groceries out by train and would immediately sell out on the platform. The first licence to sell intoxicating liquor was held by Mr Andy Jones, who ran the Railway Refreshment Rooms. Stocks were kept cool in a large cellar under the station office." This drinking arrangement continued until 1925 when a hotel was built in the town.

The scrubby land was thrown open for settlement in 1910 with the terms of settlement being that the land was to be held under licence for six years, after which time a lease could be obtained at sixpence per acre a year. The uncertain light rainfall, the intense heat, the dust, the mallee stumps, the crude farming methods, and lack of capital made farming here a hazardous concern from the beginning. In 1912 the rains did not come until 10 June; 1913 the harvest was poor, and in 1914 came "the big drought." The log tanks built underground by the battlers dredged up water but in the main, most of the water that kept the settlers alive came by train from "down the line" at Lake Hattah. Those settlers who hung on and got a crop in again were rewarded in 1917 with a bumper yield. Before the year was out, there were 137,000 bags of wheat stacked in the railway yards at Underbool.

The settlers turned their hand to anything they could find in that arid area. They harvested salt at near-by Pink Lakes, and when the sandy tracks would no longer take wagons, they carted it to the railway station at Underbool by camel team. And this was 1922, the age of the motor car in less primitive areas. Afghan camel teamsters came down from Broken Hill with their strings of camels looking for work. Railheads around the continent that needed camel teams to take over their freight were growing less and less. The Mallee was one of the last areas where the "prairie schooners" plodded to the railhead.

Even photographers were caught in the spell of the railways. This early postcard was deliberately distorted as a novelty

The Engineer-in-Chief's branch of the Victorian Railways in 1862. The locomotive is a class J 2-2-2, first introduced in 1860

NINETY-FIVE PER CENT MEN;
FIVE PER CENT IRON

An AMERICAN RAILROAD man made a remark to Harold (later Sir Harold) Clapp, Commissioner of Railways in Victoria during the depression years, which the Commissioner never forgot. "The railway is ninety-five per cent men and five per cent iron," the American said.

Clapp repeated this often to his senior officers and to the men themselves. "The railway is as strong as the men who work for it. The rank and file reflect the spirit and calibre of the men at the top."

A peculiarity of railway men is their loyalty, a sense of responsibility and affection for the track, the engine, the signal lamp, the waybill, and the surveyor's instruments. It is a loyalty that swept up and down through the ranks, from the Commissioner to the "nipper" boiling the billy beside the track.

The railway had a romance, a fascination for the technically and mechanically minded. The complex organisation, operation, and constant developments excited the mind of all who touched it.

To us now, the first railways seem to have belonged to a time remote from our own, because they brought to the economic and social life of the world changes so far-reaching that the world was never the same again. Their coming in Australia was related to the aggressive, thrusting spirit of the times that settled this land, a symbol of change as modern as moon-shots are today.

"It may be considered old-fashioned today, but there is no doubt that we felt we were taking part in a great national movement. We were very proud to be railway-men," George Williams, driver on the central desert lines for his whole working life, said in 1966. "Behind the locos and tracks and all the other paraphernalia are the men who have a vision. They have a sense of team work for collective, not individual, profit, and the vision is their country's full development."

The men were not the type to provide only a service, even a good service; that, in itself, would imply aloofness of a mere utility without a soul. They had a soul and a humour that was legendary. They wrote poems like other men wrote cheques. Some wrote hundreds. W. C. Robinson of the South Australian Railways was one of these prolific rhymists of the rails, and so was Tom Casey of Queensland.

Casey was a loco driver from steam days and was famous for his habit of writing a poem after he had put in his report at the end of each trip. "A man could only put official stuff in a report. When I'd got that away I'd sit down at one of the typewriters in the office and write what really happened."

When the diesels were introduced after the second World War, Tom and his mates were sent to test loads on the new line from Townsville to Mt Isa. The drivers must avoid "surge" with these loads of 820–1,200 tons—a lurch that could "break" the train in two. Here are two of Tom Casey's unofficial reports of two such trips—one with 820 tons, Rockhampton to Mt Isa; the other 1,260 tons, Collinsvale to Merinda.

Sir Harold W. Clapp, Commissioner of Railways in Victoria, at the controls of a diesel named after him

Thrills and Spills

We started for the Towers at 4 a.m.
In the early hours of morn.
Well, I suppose this is for what
Loco Men were born.

24D. with an English Electric
A load of 820 tons
We had not gone far along the track
When the first of our troubles begun.

We went through old Stoney with brake applied
Yet there was surges one two three
We then realised from those little kicks
What the rest of the trip would be.

Along the flats to Woodstock
The run was pretty good
From there we rode the engine
"Get Surges?" we knew we would.

At Kopi we had trouble
The surge was plainly seen
Although we carried out the instructions
In W.H.B. Fourteen.

Going down to Cardington I thought
We had it in the bag
When we broke a bloody coupling
Going through a sag.

In passing through old Oakey Creek
We tried something new
Low speed brakes on accelerate through
We stuck, blimey another blue.

We dragged her through Deep Creek
Without the brake applied
The grade it was sufficient
To keep her stretched to the other side.

It was a different tale at Spring Creek
About the 46 mile
We tried the same at Oakey
And there we stayed awhile.

We rode her with the brakes applied
Through Old Bogan's Gully
No Jockey done a better job
Not even Athol Mulley.

Up the range we brewed the tea
And partook of a meal
With something inside the tummy
Well sorta better do you feel.

From Ningela it was on again
Like a ship before a gale
We tried everything we knew
But every sag told its tale.

And then our dear old Guard complained
And finally gave us the slip
Said he was not like a good Sea Captain
Who would go down with his blooming ship.

Above: *The Williamstown workshops, Victoria, in 1870.*

Below: *The carriage makers, at Williamstown, in 1883*

I was born in the good old Towers
Many long years ago
To return to the town of your birthplace
Is a thrill that we all know.

I was never so pleased to see the Towers
With its Mullock heaps and Hills
As I was on that Friday morning
After a trip of Thrills and Spills.

Another Test

When Kostie came from Ipswich to make another test,
From Collinsvale to Merinda, we thought it would be best

To get all the facts and figures and check them over again,
Before giving a final decision for such a long and heavy train.

We started out on Sunday night—not much of a time to go,
We would have sooner watched TV in case you want to know.

Our Engineer he went along to see how it would work;
When conditions are so very tough from them he does not shirk.

Cornkelly also was on the job as well as Casey too;
When things get so very rough they know just what to do.

All went up to midnight when the driver with a wail,
Said he had just ran through water and the Mail was on our tail.

The Boss he checked the water, Kostie supplied the Rule,
Said Boss, "You can't do much with this, It's an awful bloody tool."

He then stepped into the water with feet so very bare,
Summed up the situation and knew how we would fare.

Then back to stop the Mail we went, was walking with the shakes,
One eye was on the water—the other looking out for snakes.

The guard, he said not to worry, "the flood has just begun,
Since we have been here I have only seen just one."

It seemed so doubtful if we would get there or not;
And I listened to the comments from the comforts of my cot.

The Boss then returned and said, "Me lads, it's time to go,
I've suffered some little damage, a cut foot and busted toe."

On our way again we went, at Merinda we did awaken
And had no trouble, you can be sure, to consume some eggs and bacon.

The run to Collinsvale was good, in the van, and quite so dry,
Of course, we all dozed off a bit, even you and I.

We had some biscuits and a cuppa, to help us on our way,
That's all we had to keep going on, till the finish of our day.

At last the train was ready, gauges tested front and back;
We were ready to test 1,260 tons on the Collinsvale-Merinda track.

The rain it still was falling down, when we were ready to go,
And to give the driver right away, we had to use a radio.

Away we went right up the hill—only one surge to Briaba
Where Kostie issued his instructions, on that radio he did yabber.

The run down hill was going good for a while after we started;
But before we reached the Bogie that bloomin' train had parted.

Away we went through mud and slush and spear grass four feet high,
To ascertain the damage and fix it, we would try.

Instructions passed from back to front, on our two-way radio,
Thanks to this new invention we were soon ready again to go.

That train was put together, though the engine we could not see,
Those wagons came together as gentle as could be.

Then through the Bogie and Binbee and heading for Armuna,
By the look of gauge down the range we'd be there very much sooner.

We were trusting to those brakes which at last began to grip;
You could see relief on the Boss' face, I don't think he enjoyed the trip.

When at the bottom of the range, the gauge again showed zero,
To get out and effect repairs one had to be a hero.

That train it was across a creek, the banks were very high;
With a wide stream at the bottom, no chance of keeping dry.

Well, we viewed the situation and got our eyes upon a log,
Lying across the flooding creek and we negotiated that bog.

Then up the bank the other side, which was so very much higher,
We also had to cross a fence constructed of barbed wire.

Fireman and guard carried out repairs, assisted by the Boss and I,
While Cornkelly and old Kostie stayed on the loco, high and dry.

Once again the train was joined up by the use of radio.
Our appreciation of those instruments is certainly hard to show.

Although those upon the engine said they could not understand the Irish brogue,
That's the opinion of Cornkelly, but he's such a bloody rogue.

On arrival at Merinda, it did not take long to make
A fair dinkum good old Aussie feed of potatoes and rump steak.

This was where we showed our skill—says Kostie, "Blimey, mate,
It's a pity you did not leave some room for the gravy on my plate."

Not to make any more comments I think would be the best;
I don't want to upset the gang as there is to be another test.

*   *   *   *

There was always variety, always change, always something to talk about. Jim Walsh, ganger for his working life on the Western Australian Government Railways, worked on most of the Government owned tracks. He said, "How impressions of a place change. I first went to Cue on the Murchison in March 1939. I was sent there to relieve the Inspector of Per Way. The Murchison was then experiencing a drought, everything was bare, even the mulga was dying off. My impression was that it was the country that God had forgotten.

"In 1942 I was again sent there as Inspector. The night I arrived there it started to rain. Next afternoon reports of washaways started to come in. The railway then ran as far as Wiluna, whereas now only to Meekatharra. Also Magnet to Sandstone which has now been pulled up. Well, I don't think I have ever seen so much water in my life except in the ocean. One place near Cue, at a place called Nathan, there was five feet of water above rail level. Washaways extended from Magnet to Sandstone, Magnet to Wiluna. In some instances when we had temporary repairs made, more rain came and washed them out again. We were twenty days before we got a passenger train through to Wiluna.

"It has often been said that more work was done in the Pub on weekends, than done on the track the whole week. One Saturday morning as I was making my way to the local where two gangers from outlying fettling camps were holed up, I met the local Station Master coming out from there. This is what he said to me, 'For Christ's sake, Jim, don't go in there. The bar counter is stacked up with sleepers and there are nails coming out of the windows and doors. Already about ten men have been trampled.' So they were evidently doing their job."

And for variety, few could beat Mr Charles Dunstan. He was born on 6 January 1871—ten years after the Burke and Wills expedition set out—and started work at the Melbourne Goods Shed in 1887. He is a link with the days of kings and emperors. Queen Victoria was then the sovereign of an empire "on which the sun never set," a Kaiser was in Berlin, and a Tsar ruled Russia.

A year after young Charles began at the Goods Sheds, applications were called for a job at Echuca Wharf. Twenty-three applied, but having superior qualifications, he received the appointment. "It meant a big rise," recalled Mr Dunstan, "from £65 a year to about £156."

Echuca, in those days, was a busy port through which poured the produce of the Riverina and northern Victoria. After Melbourne, it was Victoria's busiest port. At the wharf, the railways employed gangs of labourers to transfer goods between the

Above: *A ballast train gang. "Some fellas couldn't shovel salt on a boiled egg," the navvies said of the train crews.*

Below: *A fettling gang on the northern Queensland Railways leaving the depot for today's repair job*

Above: *Horses hauling scoops to form an embankment for the eastern section of the Trans-Australia line, 1912-17.*

Below: *Pay Day at Yallourn cutting, Victoria, 8 July 1921*

steamers, barges, and the train. A fleet of up to forty steamers traded along the Murray from Echuca to South Australia, and into New South Wales along the Darling, Murrumbidgee, and Edwards Rivers.

In 1888, at the start of the busy season, Charles arrived at that bustling railhead. The busy Superintendent looked the seventeen years old youth up and down, and exploded. "I asked for a man and they've sent me a boy."

He took the lad to the 1,000 foot long wharf, and pointed to steamers and barges tied up waiting discharge of their cargoes, mainly wool. "There's five thousand bales of wool to be unloaded. Do you think you can manage that?" he asked. "Well, I'll try," was the modest reply.

Undeterred by the magnitude of his new task, the youthful Dunstan arranged for overtime to be worked. "We had forty casual labourers, two tally clerks, and a foreman who was deaf. On overtime they usually worked from five in the morning till ten at night. The casuals were paid one shilling an hour—nothing extra for overtime."

More steamers were arriving as the old ones were unloaded, but by the time the Superintendent paid his next visit, all the wool had been cleared. The "boy" had proved himself as good as any man.

"The railways collected stevedoring charges of two pence a bale of wool. Each steamer carried about forty or fifty bales, and hauled a barge carrying 1,000 bales. There was a crew of five men on the steamer and one on the barge. They could go over 1,000 miles up the rivers, as far as Bourke," said Mr Dunstan, the figures tripping off his tongue as easily as though they related to the last year instead of the last century.

"Altogether, we took in about 90,000 bales of wool each season, and thousands of bales of hides and skins, as well as fruit from Mildura. On the return from Echuca, the steamers would load up with stores for the stations. They had to order supplies for a year, as the rivers were only navigable for six months.

"We loaded about 60,000 bales of wool a year, from the Murrumbidgee area, and about 20,000 bales each from the Edwards and Darling rivers. But," he chuckled, "wool from the Darling river was not very popular with the men. No one liked handling it, as it stank of camels—the plodding camels that had carried it on their backs from the sheep stations to the steamers.

"There were about forty-three rough and tumble pubs at Echuca in those days, open till midnight or later."

"Ah!" we interjected, scenting some colourful stories, "there must have been some wild nights at those grog shanties—a few fights, eh?"

"No," he replied, shattering one of our cherished illusions, "the men from the steamers and the town were generally well behaved."

It was evident that Mr Dunstan's ideas of staff management were far ahead of his time. "I always found that treating the men well gave the best results," he said. On one occasion he was asked by a supervisor why he had never reported any of the men under his charge. "Because I don't need to—they do a good job, as they're treated fairly," was the reply.

Above: *A gang of navvies at work on a cutting about the turn of the century.*
Below: *Today's gangers use a sleeper renewal machine which makes light work on the track near Mount Isa, Queensland*

He became Officer-in-Charge of Echuca Goods, and remained there till 1913. Later he was Chief Booking Clerk at Geelong, and Chief Clerk in the Maryborough District Superintendent's office.

"I always found railway work very congenial," said Mr Dunstan, drawing reflectively on his cigar. "In fact, I enjoyed working in the Department." He proudly added that, during his entire forty-nine years' service, he had worked under direct supervision for only about three years. He is the brother of a former Premier of Victoria, and the father of two sons who were in the Department—Vernon (former Acting Chairman of the Staff Board), and the late Albert, who was Assistant Staff Clerk in the Way and Works Branch.

Some of the stories telling of their concern for the public who used the railways are charming. Gavan Duffy, the Victorian lawyer and rail enthusiast, when travelling in New South Wales told of a guard who brought water to their train passengers. "Between Hill Top and Colo Vale we were astonished when the train stopped and the guard poked his head in and asked if we would like a drink, which we most cordially agreed to as the day had got very hot. We discovered that the driver was busy ladling out drinks from a mineral spring bubbling from the side of the cutting— and very nice too. After the House had shouted we went on our way again and stopped at Colo Vale, which boasts a porter who, with the rest of the population, was on hand to receive the billy of spring water that had been thoughtfully brought in for them."

Also in New South Wales, Pat Wessell, Station Master on many an outback line, said: "A country S.M. looked after the people. You couldn't be an eight to five man if you were S.M. in the bush. You opened any hour of the day or night they were able to get in. You heard a buggy or a jinker or a dray or an old car come rattling up in the middle of the night and you were getting dressed by the time they knocked on the door. And then they usually stopped for a yarn before they set off for home.

"When they had machinery broken you did everything you could to get the replacement for them. And they were good to us in return. Some of the places I've been S.M. we'd go out to the cattle stations after dark and have a swim in their overhead tank. At Walgett I remember fettlers would take mail and supplies out to settlers. The men on the land were battling in those days and the fettlers knew it. But then you'd hear that the fettlers had a surprise batch of scones delivered at their trolley shed one day. Little things, but very warm things. Of course, if a man stuck to the rules book he wouldn't get anywhere. They say that the railwayman who never broke a rule is the one out looking for a job. That's right, too."

Reading the Sydney Railway Rules and Regulations to be observed by Officers and Men employed on the Sydney Railway, one wonders how they did manage to interpret the rules at all. Dated September 1855, the "rules" had been taken over complete from the Eastern Counties Railways of England. Edmund Herald, one of the first six station masters in New South Wales, had been with that line in England, and, being the only Station Master with experience in the Colony, he presented the R. & R. book of his old firm for use in Australia.

RULE VII: Passengers are not allowed to ride on the outside or top of carriages.

RULE VIII: When the train is in motion the Guard shall keep a good look out, and note any irregularity in the running, any particular oscillation of a Carriage or Waggon, or any Signal made by a Passenger; and be at all times prepared to communicate with the Fireman, which they must do by motion with a Red Flag or Lamp, or if absolutely indispensable, by getting to the Engine; and they are desired to look back at Gatemen, Policemen and Platelayers, to see if they observe anything wrong in the passing Train.

RULE IX: Guards shall constantly keep a look out especially as to fire.

RULE X: Guards are forbidden to pass over the tops of the carriages when in motion without the most urgent necessity.

RULE XI: In case of a sudden emergency the enginemen will give two short sharp whistles when Guards must immediately apply their Brake and do all they can to stop the train.

RULE XXV: Every Ganger is required to order off all persons trespassing within the Fences, and if such persons persist in remaining, he is to take them to the nearest Station, and give them into the charge of the Station Master or the Police.

By Order of the Commissioner for Railways,
CHARLES J. NEALDS
Secretary

Sydney, 11th September, 1855.

CHRISTMAS ON THE RAILWAYS
[Composed and illustrated by the Adbhoys]

Oh Yes! I enjoy the Christmas
(Number seven platform Ma'am)
What a time for us poor porters!
(Must have a ticket for the pram)
You can see the crowds were getting
(Yes Sir—on the other side)
Never saw so much dashed luggage
(Hi Miss! yer parcels come untied)
I tell you Christmas time's a snorter
For the poor old railway porter.

Did you ever see such pushing?
(No son—I can't see yer mother)
Why do people have such luggage?
(No—you'll have to buy another)
Here they come all hot and sticky
(All aboard please! Right away)
Kids and cases—bags and babies
(Special trains the other way)
I love Christmas time—I oughter
All these years a railway porter!

Oh I'll have some Christmas dinner
(No Ma'am must be running late)
Sitting on a pile of boxes
(Woop Woop? Yes sir—Number eight)
Lucky if I grab a sandwich
(One side please—now mind your feet)
And a cup of tea—that's Christmas
(Stops two minutes at Yaapeet)
Stuck among the bricks and mortar
That's Christmas for a railway porter.

Did you ever see such crushing?
(Dogs must travel in the van)
There are thousands leaving Melbourne
(I aint seen yer brother Dan!)
Hopes you have a pleasant journey
(No Ma'am goes express right through)
Have a good blow-out on pudding
(Thanks I don't mind if I do)
And thank the Lord you've got a daughter
'Cause she won't be a railway porter.

TEN MINUTES FOR REFRESHMENTS

I heard someone call her Jessie,
Perhaps 'twas Mister Spiers, the lessee.
And her diamond eyes were twinkling,
Just like the evening star.
I found this pretty dame.
Made love to all that came,
In a quiet sort of way.
With her eyes so soft and bright;
She had lovers half-a-score,
Always some one to adore,
From the first train in the morning,
Till the last train out at night.

Spoken—Yes, her admirers were—
    A Tinker and a Tailor, and a Soldier and a Sailor,
      And a Swell who us'd to talk about his pa and his ma,
    A Butcher and a Baker, and a quiet looking Quaker,
      All courted pretty Jessie at the Railway Bar.
The Railway Songster (1896)

Above: An English Electric AIA-AIA diesel electric, perhaps the most popular of the early diesels. The one pictured was introduced in 1951 in South Australia for country work, and similar types were seen on the Commonwealth and all State lines except Victoria and Tasmania.

Below: A narrow gauge train with a trailing bauxite ore load of 4,640 tons, powered by two D class Clyde-GM diesel electrics on the Jarrahdale to Kwinana line, Western Australia. The 2,200 h.p. locomotives are the most powerful narrow gauge units.

Above: *Rail cars were introduced on suburban and country lines in the 1920s. Pictured is one of Brill's Model M55, seen for over forty years on South Australian country and suburban lines, and clocking nearly a million miles in this period.*

Below: *Carriages come in all shapes and types, and are a study in themselves from State to State. Those pictured were manufactured in the early 1900s for suburban use on the South Australian Railways, and repainted cream and green for the Centenary Year, 1936.*

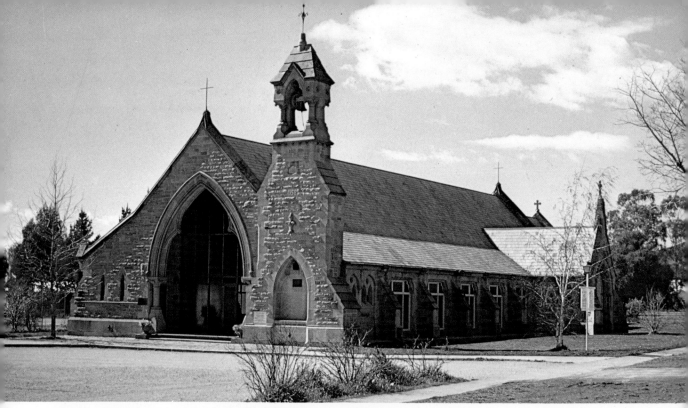

Above: *All Saints' Church of England, Ainslie, Canberra, was originally No. 1 Mortuary Station at Rookwood Cemetery, New South Wales. The Gothic-like structure was erected in 1868 (see page 59) and when the stonework was removed to Canberra in 1958 only one stone was damaged.*
Below: *The centre aisle now replaces the single track, and pews replace the platform. The two offices of the stationmaster are now used as vestries. This unique railway station is now preserved and used for public worship*

A double-headed freight train on the Trans-Australian Railway. The first locomotive is the original GM/12 Co-Co 1750 h.p. diesel electric, manufactured by Clyde-GM and capable of eighty-nine m.p.h.

Above: *A diesel-hauled passenger train of the Victorian Railways crosses the viaduct at Malmsbury.*

Below: *Victorian locomotive K173 is given a ride on the turntable. Diesels have now made turntables obsolete.*

Above: *A complex section of the suburban Victorian Railways system, showing an electrified passenger train, affectionately known as a "rattler." Australia's first electric train ran in Melbourne on 28 May 1919.*

Below left: *An Australian Railway Historical Society special at Adelaide Station, hauled by two Rx class locomotives.*

Below right: *A suburban diesel rail car unit pulling older-type carriages, South Australia.*

ENGINE 526 Z
THE FIRST ENGINE BUILT AT NEWPORT WORKSHOPS
IN SERVICE 30-6-1893

Compiled & drawn by
L.J.Harrigan, C.R.Ransford & E.Clarke
1947

Above and below: *Z class locomotive No. 526, the first engine built at the Newport work-shops, Victoria (1893). It was converted for use as a locomotive crane in 1904*

Women have always played a part in keeping the railways in operation. Above: *Newport workshop dining-room, Victoria*

Below: *The laundry section of the Victorian Railways in 1912*

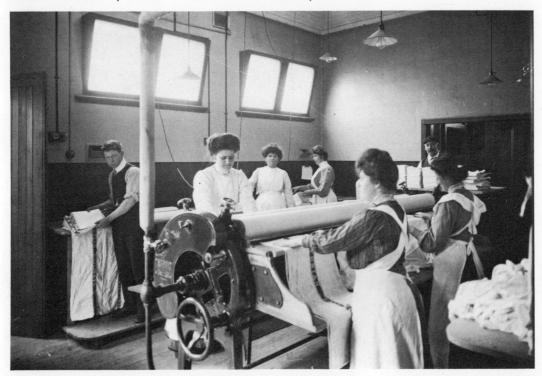

Above: *The first locomotive made at Williamstown workshops, Victoria, in 1871, seen here in 1903 hauling the Commissioner's tour train at Warragul in the Gippsland area.*
Below: *The navvies stand aside as the Adelaide to Melbourne express emerges from tunnel No. 5 in the Adelaide Hills*

In the same year as passengers were singing of the charms of Jessie at the Railway Bar, the Time Table of the Victorian Railways listed schedules for "Refreshment Room Stations."

SET-TABLE ROOMS—Spencer Street, Seymour, Benalla, Warragul, Kyneton, Bendigo, Maryborough, Geelong, Ballarat, Ararat, Stawell, Horsham, and Serviceton.

COUNTER-REFRESHMENT ROOMS—Wangaratta, Woolonga, Wahgunyah, Shepparton, Prince's Bridge, Dandenong, Korumburra, Traralgon, Sale, Woodend, Castlemaine, Echuca, St Arnaud, Kilmore, Korong Vale, Mitiamo, Hamilton, Colac, Williamstown, and Bacchus Marsh.

At the Set-table rooms the Lessee will, on arrival and departure of all passenger trains during the day or night, have Set-tables ready as per Schedule No. 1; and will also provide Counter Refreshments as per Schedule No. 4; and Sundries at Counter, as per Scheule No. 5. He will also provide Refreshment baskets. The Baskets to be supplied with refreshments, as per Schedule No. 3, and be in readiness for all passenger trains during the day and night. Empty baskets to be returned free by any guard or porter to whom they may be handed by passengers; or by the Station-masters when trains are examined. At the Counter Refreshment-rooms the Lessee will have refreshments, as per Schedule Nos. 4 and 5, constantly ready for all passenger trains during the day or night.

SCHEDULES

No. 1

Set-Table Meal

Bill of Fare—Charge 2s 6d.

Soup and Hot Joint—Beef, Mutton, Lamb, Pork, or Entrées, and Pastry; also Potatoes with Parsnips, Carrots, Beans or other Vegetables in season; Fresh White and Brown Bread; Butter and Cheese, and Marmalade; Salad, Pickles, Lettuce, Celery, or Tomatoes; Ice, during the hot season; and large cup of Tea or Coffee. In lieu of the Joint—Chops, Steaks, Ham and Eggs, Sausages, Cold Ham, Potted Salmon, or Preserved Meat must be supplied when ordered. At some rooms 1s 6d. is charged for a Set Table Meal, Entrées and Pastry not being supplied, and at most of them a glass of best Victorian Ale may be obtained in lieu of the large cup of Tea or Coffee if desired.

Table Napkins either of Linen or Paper.

No. 3

Contents of Refreshment Basket

Bill of Fare—Lessee to provide as under—Charge 3/-.

Contents—Half a chicken. Two slices of Ham or Ox Tongue. Two breakfast Rolls of Fresh White or Brown Bread. Butter and Cheese 1½ ounces of each. Pint bottle of English Ale or Porter, Victorian Ale or Lager Beer; Victorian Claret; Hock or other Native Wine; bottle of Lemonade, Tonic Water or Soda Water; or fresh Milk at choice of purchaser. A small quantity of Celery, Lettuce or Tomatoes. Pepper and Salt, Mustard and Vinegar. Two paper Table Napkins.

The Lessee to be responsible for keeping the Baskets and its fittings wholesome and bright.

No. 4
Counter Refreshments
Charge 1s.

Soup; Irish Stew; or Grilled Chop or Steak; or Stewed Steak; or Grilled Pork Chop; or Ham or Bacon and Eggs; or Sausages; with the above, Potatoes, baked and boiled; Fresh White and Brown Bread; Butter and Cheese; half-a-pint Imperial measure of best Victorian Ale; or full half-pint wine measure of Victorian Claret, Hock or other light Native Wine; or half-pint of Fresh Milk; or large cup of Tea or Coffee.

No. 5
Sundries at Counter

Sandwiches, Ham or Beef, full slices of Bread over ordinary Loaf	6d.
,, ,, above cut in half ,, ,, ,,	3d.
Tea, large cup	3d.
Coffee ,, ,,	3d.
Bread and Butter	3d.
Bread and Cheese	3d.
Bun, Roll or Seed Cake	2d.
Glass of Fresh Milk	2d.

Liquors, Cigars, Etc.

Victorian Ale or Porter, Imperial half-pint	3d.
English ,, ,, ,, ,,	6d.
Spirits per glass	6d.
Aerated Waters, per bottle	6d.
Glass of Fresh Milk	2d.
English Ale or Porter, per large bottle	1s. 6d.
,, ,, ,, ,, small ,,	1s.
Victorian Wine, per large bottle	2s. 6d.
,, ,, ,, small ,,	1s. 6d.
Victorian Ale, per large bottle	9d.
,, ,, ,, small ,,	6d.
Cigars—Havannah 6d. Swiss 9d. Cheroots 3d.	

Women were always a part of railway working but they had hurdles to clear. In 1891 an anonymous correspondent wrote to the Victorian Railways Gazette, concerning "Women In Charge Of Stations." "During a recent trip over the country lines I was surprised to notice the great number of Station Mistresses there are in the Department. On one line in particular, out of eight stations five of them are under the charge of women, most of whom have husbands earning good wages, some of them being gangers in receipt of nine shillings per day. At one station on the Heidelberg line, not long since, there was and probably is, a Station Mistress who had an assistant and a porter under her. I do not consider it right that such a state of things should exist while there are a number of competent men in the department who have seen years of service, and are no higher up the ladder now than when they started. If this sort of thing is allowed, we will probably soon have women engine-drivers, guards, and porters. If any action taken by the Traffic Union became the means of doing away with this evil, they would have the thanks of hundreds of railway men. Hoping that an abler pen than mine will take this matter up,——I am, etc.——Transit." (Note: Women were paid one shilling a day for "keeping the gates!")

By the mid-1920s the Victorian Railways alone had 130 women office workers and 500 girls in the Refreshment Rooms Service Branch. As well, there were 326 station-caretakers (virtually station mistresses), all but twelve of them in the country. There were thirty Assistant Gate Keepers (Assistants only in the sense that they were paid an assistants rate: they were the *only* keeper at the gate).

Trainee enginemen at work in the East Perth locomotive depot, Western Australia

Above: *Inspection day at signal Box A, Flinders Street, Melbourne, in 1907.*
Below: *Hand signals are necessary if visibility is reduced below 400 yards. An early photograph on the electrified system in Melbourne*

WHAT KNOW THEY OF SIGNALLING?

THE LAYMEN'S LACK of understanding of the complications of signalling is queried by "The Signaller's Lament" in the words: "What know they of signalling, Who only signal boxes know?"

From the train, the signal box appears to be a mysterious building where shadowy figures are seen dimly through walls of glass, moving leisurely behind a line of shining levers. The layman who spends an hour in a busy box during peak traffic quickly revises his ideas about the work that goes on there.

Old hands say that the more the layman knows about signals, the less he knows about them. If he can rest content with a vague knowledge of the different positions of the signal arms, and an appreciation of the significance of red, green, and yellow lights, the whole thing seems reasonably simple and straightforward. It is the rash attempt to progress from the kindergarten stage to the higher realms that bring perplexities crowding in. From then on nothing is simple.

A bewildering collection of home signals, repeater signals, disc signals, and advance starting signals are spread before your eyes. Bell codes ring shrilly in your ears, mechanical and electrical interlocking nips your incautious fingers, complications trip your feet, and a blanket of bewilderment wraps around your head. It is as well at this stage to retreat to your former state of happy vagueness.

If you stay, be content to know one thing, that though you won't understand it, you'll be seeing one of the most remarkable action-studies of our time—railways or otherwise.

Climb a score of steps to E Box, Jolimont, one of the busy signal boxes in Flinders Street Yard, Melbourne, and you'll find a self-contained, glass-walled island surrounded by a sea of trains, all electric nowadays. It is inhabited by four men, a self-correcting clock, sixty signalling levers, and a miscellany of winking lights, handless alarm clocks, and other unidentifiable gadgets. The men wrestle in a hearty and seemingly careless manner with the levers, while one of their mates writes impassively as though he is bored, at a table near a warming fire.

The glass windows shake with the reverberations every time a train thunders by. The wheels, hammering against the rails, leave a trembling behind, an uneasy silence. But as the roof of the guards' van slides by the floor of the signal box, one of the signalmen crashes down a lever as though he was a gunner firing a last shot at a retreating enemy.

Then he spins around and taps an omp-tiddely-omp-omp message on a bell key. "Five o'clock rush has just started," he says, "although things were actually busier a couple of hours ago when all the units were being marshalled from the yard on to their trains at Flinders Street." A bell shrilled, a phone rang simultaneously, and six levers were crashed back into upright positions at the far end of the box.

"At the present moment we are just going nice and quiet," the signalman informed me, as he bounded off to answer the phone, and crash two levers down, soothe someone who was irritable about "being blocked in number six road." He then turned to the other men, "Ten Box Hill, Albert . . . Twelve Oakleigh, Colin . . . I'll take the bush (the country train)."

There are four men in these busy boxes at peak periods. Here at E Box, Dick Woolcock, Signalman-in-charge has been in boxes for twenty-three years, Signalman Albert Atkins and Colin Rule eleven years each, and Don Patterson, a sixteen year old Block Recorder is just starting off with two months behind him. Dick, in charge, sits in front of a panel of keys, a type of morse code arrangement with other signal boxes; he is the nerve centre, a laconic, paternal old-hand that railways have been noted for in all sections. In fact, railmen often remember the old-hand who trained them more admiringly and affectionately than most remember a school teacher.

Beside Dick, the boy Block Recorder sits writing non-stop in a dozen columns spread across the page, every train, its time due, actual time, road . . . . . a scrawl, in obedience to Dick's nonchalant command: "That's the Oakleigh. On time Don. He must have come up like a rocket."

The two young signalmen "on the floor" swing down levers, pull switches, move with the grace of dancers across and over and down the box, their arms moving with rhythm and quiet strength.

Dick is on the phone. "Are you getting the 6.10 Cheltenham in ahead of the 6.10 Dandy? We've belled for it." Then, to the men on the floor, "Oakleigh away and Belgrave down. Ringwood away. Pilot into Burnley loop."

"What's all the lights flashing for?" he asks signalman Atkins. "I've won the lottery, that's what." But the lights go out. "Has he belled at 6.6 Lilly? Off the bush to the Oaks."

Then, from the floor, "Here's your pilot, Don." The pilot engine creeps by, its small light unseen by all but the signalman watching for it. Night has come on, it's early winter. Below us the crowd head for home, packed in shoulder to shoulder. Their eyes are in the evening paper, and they don't glance up at the men seeing them safely on their way. Their tense relaxation contrasts with the relaxed concentration in the box.

"Good God, what's that you're cooking now?" The peak is passing and Dick has reached over to turn the gas ring up under his stew. "Hey! mind my pasties and fish cakes in the oven." Don is young, still hollow in the legs.

Seven o'clock comes, the workers have all gone home and the big goods start to roll out, cars from G.M.H., pipes for Yallourn, empty cattle trucks "for the bush."

"7.10 Dandy on way," Don calls. The signalmen at the levers say, "Yeah? If you step out on the track it'll run over you," and the train thunders by. "Give him another Dim Sim. Hunger, that's his hang-up."

Up above the levers the big illuminated diagram is now showing almost all sections clear. Earlier, when the peak period was sending two trains a minute through, 116 an hour, the black line, indicating sections in use by trains, was moving along each of the eight tracks.

All the four signalmen had tried to make their complicated fast-moving world clear to me, but like the theme of a spirited fugue, a constant ringing of bells accompanied their cryptic remarks. Bells rang in most unexpected ways. They rang in minor keys, in crescendo effect, staccato, they rang singly, and two of them achieved together an obligato. The signalman tried to enlighten me on "Bell Codes" as he wrenched down two vertical levers and snapped three others up. "Each train has its code call. A box lets us know by bell-code what train is coming. We fix points and signals accordingly and pass the word along to the next box as soon as the train has passed. You need to know your timetable. That's the big thing in signalling. You see, you've only got two minutes headway between trains at peak times. You've got to anticipate, to know what's coming, to remember what time you've got."

Three bells rang joyously—they rarely seem to ring singly—and he answered each, then phoned. "That 33 Kew is running late;" the other men studied the clock. "We'll have to let the 35 Dandy out ahead of it. I'll ring Oaks and tell them to give it a good go so it won't hold up the Kew outside Richmond."

Coloured lights, and white lights were winking solemnly above the levers. Staring at them a layman feels almost obliged to acknowledge the dour salutations, but the signalmen run their eye along unblinkingly; walls shake to the passing of trains, eternal bells ring out, and the signalmen slam and crash levers, and the block recorder makes his ceaseless entries of train movements in the train register book. What are the lights that are winking in their white and coloured rows? "The five whites tell us whether the five platform roads which they represent are occupied or not. When the light shows it means the road is empty; when it is blotted out it means a train has passed into it. Simple."

"The coloured lights? They show us what the signal arms and lights are showing. We can't see all the signals from the box. So the lights bring the signals to the box for us. The greens show all clear, the reds are on danger."

And the glass pudding basins? "Time releases. They give a signalman, when he needs it, the opportunity of changing his mind in a safe and leisurely manner. When I give a proceed signal on an electrically operated signal, I can't change the route of the train or put my lever back to a normal position until the train has passed over that route—or, until I operate this time release. A little time hand inside the glass takes a minute to tick over and operate the release. I can then make the change, but having been compelled to wait and think cannot make rash movements. I wouldn't, for instance, move points while a train is passing over them."

And this is only the "little knowledge" that a signalman believes is as far as a layman should go. "Any more is dangerous. He'll get it wrong for sure. Even signalmen do at times!"

The great sense of responsibility the signalmen feel for their position is portrayed in the poem, "Asleep At The Switch."

> The first thing I remember was Carlo tugging away,
> With the sleeves of my coat fast in his teeth, pulling
>   as much as to say:
> "Come master awake and tend to the switch, lives
>   now depend upon you,
> Think of the souls in the coming train and the
>   graves you're sending them to;

Think of the mother and babe at her breast, think of
    the father and son.
Think of the lover, and loved one too, think of
    them doomed every one
To fall, as it were, by your very hand, into
    yon fathomless ditch.
Murdered by one who should guard them from harm,
    who now lies asleep at the switch."

I sprang up amazed, scarce knew where I stood,
    sleep had o'er mastered me so;
I could hear the wind hollowly howling, and the
    deep river dashing below,
I could hear the forest leaves rustling as the trees
    by the tempest were fanned,
But what was that noise in the distance? That—
    I could not understand!

I heard it at first indistinctly, like the rolling
    of some muffled drum
Then nearer and nearer it came to me, and made my
    very ears hum.
What is this light that surrounds me and seemed to
    set fire to my brain?
What whistle's that yelling so shrilly! Oh God!
    I know now—it's the train.

We often stand facing some danger, and seem to take
    root to the place;
So I stood with this demon before me, it's heated
    breath scorching my face,
Its headlight made day of the darkness, and glared
    like the eyes of some witch;
The train was almost upon me before I remembered
    the switch.

I sprang to it, seized it wildly, the train dashing
    fast down the track.
The switch resisted my effort, some devil seemed
    holding back;
On! On! came the fiery-eyed monster, and shot by
    my face like a flash;
I swooned to the earth the next moment, and
    knew nothing after the crash.

I fancied I stood on my trial, the jury and judge
    I could see.
And every eye in the court-room was steadfastly
    fixed upon me.
And fingers were pointing in scorn till I felt
    my face blushing red,
And the next thing I heard were the words "Hung
    by the neck until dead."

Then I felt myself pulled once again, and my hand
    caught tight hold of a dress,
And I heard, "What's the matter dear Jim! You've
    had a bad nightmare I guess."
And there stood Maggie, my wife, with never a scar from
    the ditch—
I'd been taking a nap in my bed and had not
    been asleep at the switch.

The layman's view of the signal box as the express speeds past

Father Christmas arrives by train on the Commonwealth Trans-Australia line, part of the special Christmas "Tea and Sugar" train

IT'S HO! FOR THE RAILWAY INSTITUTE

A SONG, ESPECIALLY COMPOSED for the occasion, was sung with gusto when the Victorian Railway Institute was opened on 22 January 1910. The song was composed by F. B. Smith and J. W. Newington.

> It's Ho! for the Railway Institute,
> A haven of peace and rest,
> Where friendship and happiness intertwine,
> And the boys are all of the best.
> Where the hand you grip is a comrade's,
> Where every man is white,
> The Victorian Railway Institute
> Is the place for me tonight.

The activities at the Railways Institute in each State were of such magnitude that no other such workers' club could equal it.

In the midst of the Depression, 1932, the Victorian Railway Institute annual report stated that they held regular old-time dances, concerts, "smokoes," and had a Table Tennis Club, Swords Club, Ice-Skating, Swimming, Golf, Rifle Clubs. They had their own recreation ground at Royal Park, the V.R.I. Ground, with cricket field, football ground, hockey field, running track with cinder foundation, scientifically drained, and equipment for jumping and hurdling for members of the Institute's Athletic Club to train for the Victorian Amateur Athletic Association summer track season.

There were tennis courts, four asphalt and covered courts, grass courts for ladies, basketball courts, a club house with locker and "shower-bath" facilities. 500 trees and shrubs had been planted to beautify the picnic area. The V.R.I. Women's Athletic Club was also active.

At the gymnasium, boxing, wrestling, and physical culture came to a peak. This year (1932) the Australasian Amateur Championships were held in Melbourne and one Institute member in the lightweight division became Australian champion and another was runner-up. Three wrestlers won their divisions, becoming Australasian champions. It was the first time in the history of interstate boxing and wrestling competitions that such a record had been achieved by the students of one gymnasium. Gymnasium fees also were "rearranged to meet the existing conditions, and are now payable in instalments."

"Social attainment classes were continued throughout the year, and although the prevailing depression, with its consequent reduction in income of all members, affected the attendance at each of these classes they were, considering all things, satisfactory." The classes were arranged for a variety of subjects, including singing, piano, steel guitar, banjo-mandolin, ukelele and violin; dramatic art, elocution, and public speaking; dancing, two-step, ballroom, and eurythmic exercises. "The fees charged and hours are arranged to meet the circumstances and requirements of students."

Some of the services available to railway institute members as advertised in the South Australian Railways Institute magazine

The Victorian Railway Institute Symphony Orchestra celebrated its tenth birthday on 1 July 1932 with thirty-eight players. There was also a V.R.I. Junior orchestra, a Victorian Railways Military Band, and a Newport Workshops Brass Band.

There was a V.R.I. Literary and Debating Society, and a V.R.I. Wireless Club (first formed in 1926). "Due to the depression, rationing, and dismissals in the Railway Service, it was expected that the Wireless Club would feel the strain very badly, but the Club at the end of the unfinancial year is as sound as at its inception, being probably the only active Radio Club in Victoria, if not Australia." They had their own amateur broadcast station, 3RI, with listeners "as far afield as New Guinea, New Zealand, and Queensland, as well as regular listeners in Tasmania and New South Wales."

An annual picnic had been held for the Returned Railwaymen's Social Club— with wives—to Queenscliff on a bay trip.

"In a period of financial stress and general depression, the Library has afforded members an opportunity for relaxation and recreation, and has met the need of those whose aim is to increase their technical knowledge, or is purely cultural. During the past year 7,000 members have availed themselves of their library membership. There were 2,211 enrolled in educational classes and 883 receiving correspondence in districts where the Institute is unable to provide classes."

Prizes were given to encourage the men, including the Harold W. Clapp prizes:

A Division: Station accounts and management.
B Division: Safe working (Signalling, Train Running, Guards Duties, English and Arithmetic).
C Division: Engine working and Westinghouse Brakes, plus English and Arithmetic
D Division: Railway constitution and maintenance, plus English and Arithmetic.

There was also a prize for the student who, "during the year has displayed the most persevering effort in his work."

Their own magazine was as vital as their Institute. In one issue they published Katherine Mansfield's poem, "When I was a Bird," and articles on the third Asiatic expedition of the American Museum of Natural History, having brought to Peking two dozen dinosaur eggs estimated to be 10 million years old. Articles also discussed escorted tours around the State, and the estimated value of Victorian production for the year. A children's page was livelier by far than many in today's papers. The Secretary of the Railways Carnival Committee reported handing cheques for $4,000 to Ballarat Orphanage. This secretary, Bob Cadell, was given special leave in 1926 to conduct an appeal for St Vincent's Hospital and another for the orphanage re-building fund, and brought in $2,000 for the hospital and $20,000 for the orphanage.

The magazine even tells the origin of the name of the town, Katamatite. "A very drunken surveyor staggered down to a group of men by Boosey Creek. Collectively addressing them with what was probably meant to be 'mate' but came out 'Kate', he demanded to know, superfluously, whether he was 'tight.' 'Yes,' said the men, 'You're on the Boosey.' The surveyor was so charmed with this polished wit, that he laughed and laughed. 'Kate am I tight?' he said over and over. 'Yes, you're on the Boosey!' 'Kate am I tight!' and Katamatite that place is till today."

The Locomotive Band, formed in 1883 in South Australia, and still functioning as the South Australian Railways Institute Band

Mr Curnow stops the special train just prior to the capture of the Kelly gang

SPECIAL TO GLENROWAN

ROMANTICS HAVE CLAIMED that Ned Kelly had a vast loathing of railways, that he believed their coming was an intrusion on the countryside where men could still ride wild and free. Still others claimed that Kelly, had he not turned bushranger, might have made a great general.

In the welter of words that have been written since the gang perished behind the railway station in Jones' pub, Glenrowan, it is possible to believe almost anything. If the truth is sought, it is to be seen in the archives of the State Library of Victoria where "The Kelly Papers" are held. Here among the other "Kellyana" are the reports of the Kelly Reward Board, the Government appointees who examined claimants to the reward. In the reading of these there is nothing to say as to whether Kelly did or did not loathe railways, but there is ample evidence that had he joined the army he wouldn't have gone far.

In his final escapade, Kelly did employ some strategy: his gang would murder the informer Sherritt, near Beechworth; the police would be expected to send a special train up from Melbourne; and the gang would then wreck it near Glenrowan and shoot the police as they tried to escape. On the applications for rewards, most railmen applying spoke of having been sent out on trains previous to this "following a report that the Kelly gang were out."

For several years trains had rocketed up and down the north-east of the State in search of the gang. Even the gangers along the tracks had been instructed to watch for "any suspicious characters" crossing the line, or any traces of the line having been crossed, and as early as 19 November 1878, notices had been sent out.

So Kelly had no doubt that the murder of Sherritt would bring a train up the line. What was poor strategy for him was to expect that his four-man gang could overwhelm a large body of armed police and blacktrackers after the train had been wrecked.

The documents tell, in each man's own words, of the gang's arrival in Glenrowan, of their waking the Station Master, then the platelayers, and forcing them to take up a rail a little way past the station, on a curve. Later, the gang imprisoned all the railway workers and any others they came across in the small shanty-hotel behind the navvies' tents in the railway paddock. There, in the pub, they waited for the train they knew would come.

In fact, two trains were coming. On the pilot was Driver Alder, Fireman Burch, and Guard McPhee. In December 1880, McPhee wrote to the Reward Board.

Maryborough
December 18th 1880.

Traffic Manager.
Sir,

Referring to explanation required Re the capture of the Kelly Outlaws; I would beg to state that I was awakened on the morning of the 28th July last by Mr Hollow Telegraph Operator; he informed me that Mr Stephens (Station-master) required me on duty as soon as possible.

On reporting myself ready for duty, I received instructions to proceed to Beech-worth preceding a Special Police train (Acting as Pilot). After making a start, we went along all-right till within a mile and a half of Glenrowan Station when I noticed a reddish light ahead; my first impression was that the light was caused by a burning log in the bush (a very common occurrence) and what made it appear more so, was through seeing the light almost at the place where the curve com-menced which would lead a person that knew to suppose that the light was straight ahead. Upon getting about a quarter of a mile nearer, I could see that the light was very close to the line. When about two hundred yards off, I put my head out of the side window and could distinctly see a whitish object with a light in front. I immediately applied my Brake, and just at the same moment it flashed through my mind that it was a ruse to stop the train. I then got out and stood on the sideboard of the Van until I got opposite the figure which proved to be the Schoolmaster, Mr Curnow. I jumped off saying, "Holloa mate, what's the matter?" He answered, "Kelly's," and then told me that the rails were torn up between Glenrowan Station and the Sydney Crossing. I said that must be about half a mile from the Station. He answered Yes and then told me that the Gang were in possession of Glenrowan. I, (still thinking it was a ruse) asked him his name. He did not tell me but said, I am the school teacher. I asked him if he would get in my Van. He said he could not as he had his wife to protect and that he was running a great risk to his life. (This conversation did not last two minutes.) I then went and spoke to the Driver (H. Alder) and told him what was the matter also that I was going back to stop the following train which I immediately did. I am confident I went back over half a mile. Upon getting within a few yards off the train I had stopped, I was met by Superintendent Hare and Senior Constable Kelly to whom I related the whole of the conversation I had with Mr Curnow. Supt Hare took some of his men and walked up to the Pilot Engine which by this time had rolled gently down till within a quarter of a mile of the Police train. I followed him up and, when opposite the Engine, heard Driver Alder remark to Mr Hare if it would suit to couple both trains together. Supt Hare considered some little time, and then said he thought it would be advisable. I done so, and then drew up to Glenrowan Station, and after we stopped, I was assisting the Police to discharge their horses from the trucks when Constable Bracken rushed up, saying the Gang were in Mrs Jones and for God's sake surround the Hotel. Supt Hare then sang out, "Come out Boys," and he and the Police made a rush for the Hotel. I let go the horse I was holding and followed them over. I would be about twenty yards behind the Police when the firing commenced and having no fire-arms on me at the time I thought the position I was in rather unsafe, and I made for the station again which refuge I reached in a very short time. I then watched the proceedings from around the corner of the station house until Mr Hare came up wounded. He said he required me to go to Benalla for Reinforcements. Guard Bell and I then shunted my van behind the Pilot Engine and made a start back for Benalla which place we reached in about ten minutes. I told Mr Stephens all that occurred and the orders I had received from Supt Hare and also suggested that he would send out some of the permanent way men to

Engineer in Chief's Office
Railway Department
Melbourne Nov.19 1878
(Confidential)
Memo for
Ganger S. Capp
          If you or any
of your men see any suspicious
characters crossing the line or
any traces of the line having been
crossed, except at the regular level
crossings, be good enough to
communicate full particulars to
the nearest Station Master, who
will immediately forward them
to the police

                    Robt. Watson
                    Engineer in Chief

An early memo shows the railway's desire to co-operate in the capture of the Kelly gang

repair the line. He sent for Ganger Dick who accompanied me to Glenrowan on my second trip. After reaching Glenrowan with the reinforcement I remained on the platform till Ganger Dick came back from where the Rails were torn up. He told me he wanted more men. I said I thought they were all prisoners in the Hotel but mentioned that I would go down the line towards Benalla and try and pick some up. I went about a mile (with the engine) and succeeded in getting two plate-layers whom I brought to the Station. I then asked Mrs O. Connor and her sister if they would like some refreshments. They answered yes so I went over to McDonalds Hotel and got a bottle of Brandy and a glass and whilst there met Mr Stanistreet. I asked him to come over and open the station which he did. Upon presenting the Brandy to Mrs O.Connor and sister they refused saying, "Oh no, we could not touch that." But asked if it were possible to get some sherry and milk. I think Guard Bell got that for them. I gave some of the Brandy to the reporters and others who were on the Station and then went away towards the Policemen who were surrounding the Hotel intending to empty the bottle amongst them. I had just got outside the Railway fence when Ned Kelly emerged from the bush close by. I thought the firing too warm and retired to my old position behind the station till I saw him fall. I then rushed over arriving there about fifth or sixth and the first use made of the remaining brandy was to give Ned Kelly a glass three parts full. He was then taken to the station. I followed and after reaching the station assisted Guard Bell to make up his train. He then started for Benalla, I remained behind until Ganger Dick came back and told me the line was all clear. I then proceeded to Benalla and told the station master the line was all right for 6.10 a.m. up to come on, I then received instructions to act as Pilot for all trains during the day which duty I was engaged on till 11.30 p.m. at night having been two trips to Glenrowan and three trips to Wangaratta.

I am Sir your obedient servant
Guard A. A. McPhee

Guard Bell, on the following Special, wrote to the Commissioner for Railways, the Hon. John Woods, while Driver Bowman and Fireman Hollows wrote to their Locomotive Superintendent.

Melbourne
Sept. 11 1880

To the Hon. John Wood
Sir

I respectfully place before you a statement of fact with reference to the 10 p.m. Kelly Special, which left Melbourne on the night of Sunday 27th June.

The special being ordered in a hurry, and it being Sunday, no notice could be given along the line, and it being a very dark night there was a great risk of running through some of the gates, all went well until we arrived at Craigieburne, when we ran into the Station gate, striking it end on it was a more solid obstruction and the force of the collision broke the spring hanger, tore off the step and snapping off the Gate shaft about 8 inches below the handle. The engine being thus disabled I told the driver to see if any other damage had been sustained, he informed me that he did not think so but my Brake is gone and it is not safe to proceed without it. Knowing how important the mission was, I informed the Driver that I would take all the responsibility of Engine and Train, and work both with Brake van. Had I sent the Engine back to Melbourne for a fresh one it would have caused a delay of (4) hours, and taking the time into consideration it would have brought the train into Glenrowan at daylight and by that time the Gang would likely have escaped.

Arriving at Glenrowan I found that the Station Master was in the hands of the Bushrangers, therefore I had to take charge of the Gates and shunting and displacing the Special train for reinforcement to Benalla, also instructing the Station

The railway embankment at Glenrowan where the Kelly gang had torn up the rails in an effort to derail the police train

Master at Benalla about the line being torn up on the Wangaratta side of Glenrowan. I also sent an Engine to the Platelayers about half a mile up the line to get all the hands I could to repair the line so that the 10 a.m. up from Wodonga would not be detained, I also beg to state that I did all this at the risk of loosing my life as the Bullets were flying round me in all directions as most of my work had to be done in front of Jones's Hotel I fully expected to be shot as I had to take my hand lamp to do my shunting and signal the return specials, I was a good target for the bush-ranger to fire at.

Trusting you will think favourably of this statement,

I have the honour to be,
Sir,
Your most obedient servant,
Frank Bell

The Kelly capture—Bird's-eye view of Glenrowan. 1. Jones' Hotel, 2. Out House, 3. Railway Station, 4. Station Master's House, 5. McDonald's Hotel, 6. Platelayers' tents, 7. Positions taken by police, 8. Trench: Lieutenant O'Connor and blacktrackers' post, 9. Spot where Mr Hare was shot, 10. Paddock where horses were shot, 11. Tree where Ned Kelly was captured, 12. Road to Bracken's Station, 13. Half-a-mile from here the rails were taken up

S. Mirls Esqr.,   Benalla
Loco Supt.   December

Sir,

The following is a detailed account of my trip after the Kelly gang on the 28th of June on the 27th of June about 3 p.m. I received instructions from Mr Hodgkins to get No. 107 Engine ready as the Kelly gang had broke out again and I would have to run a Special train to Beechworth with the Police after standing by with the Engine all ready when called upon, about 9.00 p.m. I received instructions from the station master to be in the yard at 12.0 p.m. to get some trucks loaded with horses for the Police as there was a special to leave Melbourne for Wangaratta at 10.00 p.m. with Black Trackers and I would have to proceed the Special from Benalla to Wangaratta as Pilot and then take the special train from Wangaratta to Beechworth as the Kellys had said they would take the line up on the arrival of the special from Melbourne about 1.30 a.m. Mr Hodgkins inform me the Melbourne engine had run through a pair of gates and carried away his Tender Brake and Halder would have to take a Brake van and run as Pilot to Wangaratta as he had no Brake power. I would have to take the Special train from Benalla to Beechworth. The Pilot left Benalla at 2.0 a.m. I left five minutes after with the Special knowing that Halder was going to run to save time I only having a 3 feet wheel I made the best time I could with safety to the Engine keeping in sight of the Pilot till coming to a corner near No. 6G gate I lost sight of the Pilot on the Bank coming near to him I saw that he was stopped thinking he was stopped by the Kellys I gave two sharp taps of the whistle as signal for the police to be on there guard I then went up towards him till I was stopped by the guard of the Pilot he said they been stopped by a *man who said the Kellys was at the Station waiting for us and the Inspector of Police and his men and they have tore the line up and the other side of the station after some Conversation between Halder and Inspector Hare three Police came on to* the Engine and all lights were put out and we were both coupled together all doors open we proceded slowly up to the station with as little noise as possible we soon arrived at the station, the Fireman *commenced before the horses were out of the trucks those that were not and bolted past the engines at the first fire. Soon the bullets were* flying over our engine after stopping for some five minutes on my engine the bullets was coming too close to me thinking we would be required any minute I got the engine ready I then went on to Alder engine it was no safer there we got under protection of the tender in a few minutes Alder received orders to go to Benalla for more reinforcements all the Points was locked at each end of the station while Halder was shunting his van front of Jones Hotel while all the Firing was going on and cut the Points to slow the engine to come through with safety shortly after I received instructions that Mr Hare had got wounded I would have to take him on the Engine and run him to Benalla for Medical treatment and return to Glenrowan at once I returned to Glenrowan at 5.30 a.m. At 8.30 a.m. I received instruction to take the special train Back to Benalla on arrival there I received Instructions from the station master to run as Pilot between Benalla and Wangaratta for the 6.10 a.m. down and 10.0 a.m. and

Kelly in the guard's van, being taken to Beechworth. When he saw the Strathbogie Ranges, he said "There they are; shall I ever be there again?"

5.5 p.m. up trains. At 7 p.m. I received instructions from the station master at Benalla that the Pilot would not be required any more.

remain Sir
Your obedient Servants
John Bowman Driver
Herbert Hollows Fireman

Driver Coleman and Fireman Stewart, coming on the scene later, brought up the reinforcements.

Benalla
Dec. 23rd/80

To the Secretary of the Kelly reward fund.
Sir

I respectfully wish to ask if there is anything to be given to the enginemen who took the Police to the scene at Glenrowan on the day of the Kelly gang capture that me and my Firemans case be entertained as we were in as much danger of being shot as anybody. We left Benalla at 5.15 and with the second batch of Police for Glenrowan arriving there at 5.45 a.m. and stayed there until about 9 a.m. during all the heavy firing. During all this we had to take the engine past the place they were firing enough to get what Platelayers we could to come and repair the line. At this time the shots where flying about in all directions, and when returning with the engine and men, I had to stop opposite the place for my mate to get down and hold the points to turn the engine into the middle road which under the circumstances was very dangerous.

We remain
Your obedient servants,
Richard Coleman (Driver)
John C. Stewart (Fireman)

Of all the railmen claiming the reward, Guard Jesse Dowsett had the most impressive achievements to present. Jesse had actually been fired at by Ned himself and had even exchanged witticisms with the bushranger in the heat of battle as he, Jesse, fired back.

Sandhurst
Dec. 16th 1880

To the Board for the Rewarding
of the capture of the Kelly Gang.
Gentlemen,

In compliance with your advertisement in *Argus* Dec 1st I wish to bring under your notice my claim to a share of the reward offered for the capture of the Kelly gang.

I may state that I was stationed in Benalla before the Kellys took to the bush and after the robbery at Euroa was in charge of several police special trains at Euroa, Wilmont, and Beechworth, which always ran late at night or early in the morning. On Sunday the 27th of June I was sent for by the station master and told to take charge of Police Special to Beechworth as the Kellys had broken out and murdered a man there. We waited all ready till after 7 p.m. the station master told me that the special would not start till we arrived from Melbourne with the trackers that would be about 1 or 2 a.m. I was sent home, but was not called. When the Melbourne special arrived about 4.30 a.m., I was called and told the Kellys with a large gang were fighting the Police at Glenrowan. I up at once and ran over just as the train was starting with Supt Sadleir in charge of more Police. We ran up to Glenrowan very quickly. On getting out of the train the firing was very brisk and as I could hear a woman screaming out not to shoot her children as they had shot the father, I ran up the bush at the back of the station and after getting to the back of the Hotel crept on my knees towards it. Not far from the back of the hotel, I saw one of the platelayers' wives, a Mrs Reardon, with a baby in her arms—she was in great danger as the bullets from both parties were flying about her but she was like one distracted. I called to her in low tones to come towards me, telling her I was the Police. She came over towards me and I caught hold of her and her baby and brought her to the station in safety. After she calmed down a bit she was able to give important information as to really who were in the house and where they were. On going back to where I had brought her from, I found that Sergeant Steele and Senior Constable Kelly had taken up a close position, commanding the back door and stables, the yard having several horses in and firing being kept up at the back, we thought they were going to make a rush for the horses so they were shot and every time a shot was fired from the back window we fired at the flash. After this had gone on for some time I saw a curious looking figure coming through the gloom making for the rear of the Hotel. I sang out to the object and Senior Constable Kelly also called out but he came on firing very rapidly till he came to clump of saplings where he seemed to be sheltered. I crept from tree to tree getting closer to him when he seemed to be reloading I fired several shots at him and could hear them ring on him. On looking back I saw Senior Constable Kelly was coming up and told him he could get a shot at him with his rifle if he came to where I was. He did so and fired twice, hitting his hand on one occasion. I got closer to him when all at once he left the saplings and came straight for me. I emptied my revolver at him not twenty yards away from him and as a proof I was hitting him, one of my bullets was found embedded in his box of cartridges, but he came on quite steadily saying fire away, you b—dy dogs, you carnt bust me. I thought it was all up with me and threw myself down at the butt of a large fallen tree, reloading as quickly as possible. On looking up I found he had walked into a trap between two large limbs of the tree I was at. I could now see Steele circling from the left and Kelly on the right, so I called out to the figure to give up so as to distract his attention from them but he said no never while I have a shot left. As I thought I had a good shot for his head, he being not more than fifteen yards off, I fired hitting him full on the head, but, not having the slightest effect on him. I said, as I fired, how do you like that; he replied, how do you like this, and leant over the log firing as he did so. I saw Steele fire twice, I think, and he seemed to fall backwards. I ran up and jumping over the log saw he and Steele on the ground. I grasped the revolver from him as he fired and Senior Constable Kelly, coming up almost at the same

Guard J. Dowsett holding the revolver he took from Ned Kelly. He is also displaying a boot and a bullet-riddled tin of ammunition which was in Kelly's possession

moment, pulled his head gear off him. Steele at once recognised him and would have shot him but I said no, take him alive. A number of people now came up, several Constables among them, and after stripping him of his armour carried him down to the station. As it was now known that Byrnes was shot, I came away to Benalla as Mr Sadleir was sending a telegram for a big gun to blow the chimney down that they were supposed to be in, though Ned Kelly repeatedly said they were not there or we would have been shot down like rotten sheep when we rushed him. This statement like many more of his proving to be false. For the truth of the above, I respectfully refer to the Reporters at the *Argus, Age,* and *Telegraph,* the Artist of the *Sketcher,* Doctor Nicholson, Senior Constable Kelly, who was close to me all the time, and the report of Superintendant Sadleir, hoping that I have not tired your patience.

> Gentlemen
> I remain yours Respectfully
> Jesse Dowsett
> Railway Guard, Sandhurst

Dowsett's part in the capture did not go unremarked by Kelly sympathisers. An article about him in 1926 records that as threats were made against Mr Dowsett, he was promoted to the position of Senior Guard in another part of the State.

His volunteering to go after the Kellys would certainly bring him into disfavour with sympathisers of the bushranger but his bravery cannot be denied. He evidently felt a strong sense of public duty and acted on it, a brave thing to do in the face of adverse public opinion. On two occasions "he ran a special" to areas where the gang had been reported; on each occasion, Kelly sympathisers had ridden ahead to warn the gang.

Dowsett, long after the end of the Kelly gang, again showed his valour, this time at Macedon. The engine had shunted the Governor's State Car into a siding when Dowsett, who was holding the points, saw the rest of the train full of passengers being blown away by the strong wind down the line towards Gisborne. He rushed to his van, but the brake was not connected, so on his hands and knees he crawled along the narrow foot boards till he got to where he could apply the brake, and so pulled up the train.

He was highly commended by the Railway Department for this action, but for his "meritorious conduct" against the Kelly Gang he was promoted "to the position of passenger guard at an increase of one shilling a day from the 1st inst. Dated 1 December 1880."

He lived until his late eighties, a spry, intelligent old man, still in possession of the revolver he took from Ned Kelly and the boot they had to cut off Kelly's wounded foot. (The revolver is now in the Historical collection, State Library of Victoria.)

Of the ninety-two claims put to the Kelly Reward Board, sixty-six were successful, among them nine railmen. Guard McPhee, Driver Alder, and Fireman Burch (of the pilot engine) £104.4.6 each; Driver Bowman, Fireman Hollows, and Guard Bell, £84.4.6 each; Driver Coleman and Fireman Stewart, £68.3.4 each; and Jesse Dowsett, the gun-carrying guard, £175.13.9.

The Board recommended five men to be considered as worthy of Special Recognition for services rendered during the period of search for the outlaws. Two of these were Station Masters, Mr Stephens (Benalla), and Mr Lang (Wangaratta). An interesting part of the reports on these two men is that they kept their telegraphs open and available to police, in contrast to the telegraph stations in their towns, which closed at certain times, and on at least one occasion during the actual final pitched battle could not be raised.

Of the other railmen involved, the platelayer, poor Martin Cherry, a very popular old man who had been born sixty years earlier in Limerick, Ireland, was wounded by police fire when being held prisoner in the hotel. He died half an hour after being carried from an outhouse. This took place after the hotel was set on fire by police. Platelayer Reardon had much to complain of. His young son had been shot through one shoulder by police and his wife had been fired on while trying to escape with her baby, putting a hole through her shawl. Constable Arthur said to Steele, "If you shoot on that woman again, I will shoot you."

The thirteen year old Johnny Jones had been shot dead before Platelayer McHugh was able to help Mrs Jones, the proprietor, out to safety.

When it was all over and the bodies of the rest of his gang were being charred in the burning hotel, Ned Kelly was lying on the floor of the railway station. "Hundreds of people had by now ridden to the scene and the platform was crowded, all straining to get a glimpse of the captured outlaw. He had five serious wounds, twenty-five minor wounds on hands, legs, and arms, his body was severely bruised from the percussion of bullets against his armour and both his legs were blackened. He was later sent to Melbourne in a guards van, no doubt shivering with Victoria's harsh winter cold which the reporters and artists had complained of when they came up to report on his activities two days before."

The township of Greta, eight miles from Glenrowan, was the home of the Kelly family during most of Ned Kelly's youth

Saltia township, north of Port Augusta, South Australia, on what was the Commonwealth Railways' line to Alice Springs

THE GREAT GUM TREE

ONE OF THE MOST poetic references on the railways in Australia was written by J. W. Gregory, Professor of Geology in the University of Glasgow. He had taken a party of geologists to the Lake Eyre Basin and Central Australia in the summer of 1901–02 when the country was in the vice of one of the worst recorded droughts. The temperature at times hit 125 in the shade. Gregory, who coined the term, *The Dead Heart of Australia,* with the title of the book he wrote of his journey, remarks on the legend of the Kurdimurka, the tribe whose mythology tells of ancestors who lived in the dry land when it was covered with great forests that reached to the sky. They lived in the tree tops until one day the succulent herbs on the ground tempted them down to earth. While they were down below their retreat was cut off by the destruction of the three gum trees which were the pillars of the sky. They were thus obliged to roam on earth, and their bones became part of the great graveyard of prehistoric bones, both of people and the extinct giant kangaroos and the mighty diprotodons that the white man now seeks. The Kurdimurka were lost forever, because their gum trees had gone.

"We had, however," Gregory writes, "the comfort of knowing that our gum tree—The Great Northern Railway of South Australia—would be ready to bring us back, as safely and easily as it was taking us to the edge of the desert we hoped to explore."

As he travelled on the Great Northern Railway to Hergott Springs, where his camels were waiting, Gregory put to paper the words that many rail men in that region had been unable to find to describe the magic they felt in their surroundings; hot, dusty, waterless, and far from home. When they spoke of the desert they said: "It gets you!" "It's beautiful." "You can't describe it." Gregory described it for them. "The desert circle spreads like the round ocean, girdled with the sky," and he read to them Kendall's lines: "And through the days when the torrid rays strike down in a coppery gloom . . . and flaming, noontides mute with heat, beneath the breathless, brazen sky."

No pool, no bush, no house is seen round the parched flats, the wastelands of eternity, the home of the dingo that made Kipling write "where the Warrigal whimpers and bays through the dust of the sere river courses."

It is a land for which there is no middle course. A man loves or loathes it.

Gregory loved it. He wrote: "On Friday, December 13, 1901, we started from Adelaide by the early morning train. Notwithstanding the hour, several of our friends came to bid us good-speed and give us their last advice and their last additional information. Our camels with the camel driver, Steer, were to meet us at Hergott Springs, some four hundred and forty miles north from Adelaide.

"The railway journey to Hergott takes two days. For most of the way the gauge of the line is narrow, and, as, owing to the great diurnal variation of temperature in this country, the rails cannot be closely laid, the speed of the trains is necessarily slow. North of Quorn, the train goes only every other day, from Hergott to Coward's Springs there is one train a week; and on the last section of the line there is but one train a fortnight.

"As we approached the end of our railway journey the heat became more intense, and we received the lugubrious sympathy of residents along the line, who came down to meet the occasional train. Some of them obviously regarded us as either ignorant of the fact that summer in the southern hemisphere occurs at Christmas, or else as not in our right minds. My apology that we were visiting the country at that time of year because it was the only time available to us was dismissed as so miserably inadequate, that I never dared to repeat it. The assertions made to us as to the fatal fury of the heat, the delicacy of the fragile camel, and the appalling scarcity of water, as well as the warnings to beware of the fate of some early explorers in the Lake Eyre basin, suggested a fresh explanation of the Kurdimurka legend. Might it not be an allegory on the experiences of Sturt and the tragic fate of Burke and Wills?

"When settlements were first founded in South Australia, men cherished the hope that beyond the waterless wastes, that lay behind the coast-lands, rose a cooler, better land, with well-watered valleys, timbered hills, and turfed steppes, by which the inhabitants of the coast-lands could cross the desert zone to the land of promise beyond. Sturt's descriptions of his sufferings were so vivid that when they reached Adelaide, they turned his wife's hair white in a single night.

"In spite of their sufferings Sturt and most of his party escaped the fate of the Kurdimurka. Burke and Wills were less fortunate. They also reached Lake Eyre basin in quest of better lands beyond the desert. They were cut off from the south by the summer, and eked out a miserable existence until death relieved their sufferings. Undeterred by fate, men have never been found wanting to continue the work, until now a well-equipped and admirably managed railway runs far out into the desert-land. Four hundred and forty miles from Adelaide, the Great Northern Railway of South Australia turns suddenly westward to cross the hills between the foot of Willoura Mountains and the southern shore of Lake Eyre. At the bend of the railway is the township of Hergott, which has grown up around a group of springs, named not by a profane German, but after their discoverer, one of the members of Sturt's second expedition.

"As we landed from the train we found the platform redolent with Afghan, impressing on us the fact that Hergott is one of the leading caravan centres in Australia: for it is the point where the main stock-route to western Queensland branches from the railway-line. Until recently all communications to the back blocks of Queensland, even the customs books and police officers, were sent from Brisbane via Melbourne and Hergott, a journey of 2,553 miles, including 330 by cart, to reach a place only 530 miles from a station on the Queensland Railways.

"The township of Hergott is small, and its few sights are quickly seen. The best view is from the verandah of the hotel; but some of my companions were certainly disappointed even with the best. The view embraces a wide tract of the flat type desert country. The first impression is of dreary monotony and aching barrenness. The ground is a waste of sand and pebbles, with an occasional bush, which appears to have escaped the voracious camel by successfully shamming death.

"But in spite of the unpromising elements in this view, it has a beauty of its own. There is a fascination in its breath. The wide plain, the low horizon, and the magnificent expanse of the sky give a sense of joyful freedom. The pure colours at dawn and sunset, the fine atmospheric effects, the thatched, mud-walled huts of the Afghan camp and its turbaned inhabitants, all give the country an Oriental aspect."

Gregory and his party safely completed their exploration and headed for "the gum tree of the Great Northern Railway." They were travelling at night to avoid the heat of the day, but must make good time if they were to connect with the train.

"So long as the moon was above the horizon we managed well: but it sank below a bank of clouds, before we were clear of the hills. We had to find our way across the great western plains in utter darkness. We made but slow progress and I was beginning to think that our guide was out of his bearings: when suddenly we stumbled across the railway line which seemed out of place in such a wilderness. We followed it for half a mile and at 2 a.m. we saw the flicker of a dying fire, which told us where the caravan was camped and our supper was awaiting us. To the cheering strains of Guy Smith's rendering of what seemed to be, a combination of the Hallelujah Chorus and the Melbourne University Anthem, we rode our camels into the Warrina station-yard.

"The fortnightly train was expected in seven hours time, so we had won the race from Kalamurina, and had finished our traverse of the hottest and dustiest depression in the hot and dusty continent of Australia."

Many men worked on the desert lines, but the only ones who stayed and made it their home were those snared by the irresistible fascination the desert has for some men. The pathless tract throws a spell over its lovers as strong as that of the sea to those who feel its pull. The two have a proverbial resemblance, so much so that even the beasts of burden of the sand hills have been known as the "ships of the desert." Those whose lodestar has been the desert can rarely describe its charm. They know man feels less fettered and freer in the desert, the world seems wider, the sky higher, and the horizon further off.

The blazing furnace of full moon brings out their loathing and some declare you must hate it before you can love it, and sometimes the two are experienced together. Love comes oftener at night when the indigo sky fairly blazes, spangled with stars bigger than you ever saw before, as though it were put there just to delight the traveller who earns delight in his travail of the day. There is absolute silence. There is a quiet when you hear the rhythm of your heart drumming on the walls of its cage. Some men believe, when they lie awake under the big stars on the desert, that the sky swings down, low, "so low you know if you reach up your arm your finger tips will be spangled with star-dust," Joe Pickford, an old Welsh ganger on the track, told me once.

The camel men Gregory referred to were invariably called Afghans or "Ghans," although only a few came from Afghanistan. Most of them were from Rajasthan and Baluchistan and the area that is now West Pakistan. Even when Turks, Persians and Egyptians were brought in, they were lumped together under the generic term "Ghans."

Gathered together at Beltana, the "Ghans" manned the greatest camel breeding stud farm in Australia. Owned by Sir Thomas Elder and Samuel J. Stukey, the

Above: *A locomotive on the North Australia Railway decorated for the annual picnic from Darwin, Northern Territory.*
Below: *Inspecting the locomotive for trouble spots, somewhere south of Darwin, Northern Territory*

Beltana camel-carting company eventually spread throughout much of central Australia. They imported dromedaries from Karachi and in this way began the nucleus of the herds that serviced the central lands and carried the inland explorers on their waterless treks.

Because of the incompatibility between horses and camels, the two were kept apart and rarely did horse teams work in the vicinity of camel teams. Camels were preferred by construction men for, even though the horse had greater speed and mobility, the camel could much more successfully withstand waterless days and indifferent food, but, most importantly, camels were far superior in strength and their endurance was legendary. Bullocks and horses could haul great loads over reasonably level surfaces where water and feed were available, but camels could cross land impassable to horses or bullocks pulling as great a load, and, as well, pack great weights on their backs.

The first great use of camels on construction work was on the building of the Overland Telegraph Line (1870-2) between Adelaide and Darwin. (From Darwin a submarine cable linked Australia to London via Indonesia and India.)

By the time railways began to push up north from Port Augusta in 1879, Beltana stud and its camels were famous. Although a few were used for hauling construction material, the greatest number were used to bridge the distance between the railhead and inland sheep and cattle runs.

The line reached Beltana from Port Augusta in 1881 and came to rest, after stopping at several railheads, at Oodnadatta in 1891. After the railway opened to Oodnadatta, a series of bad seasons was experienced in South Australia and the State did not proceed with construction. The railhead, therefore, remained at a point in one of the driest and most arid tracts of land between Port Augusta and Darwin. It did not go on to Alice Springs until 1929. Until this time the camel teams thrived. They freighted goods as far as Newcastle Waters (Northern Territory), a distance of 780 miles, at a cost of thirty-eight pounds a ton. In contrast, supplies sent from Darwin to Newcastle Waters (450 miles) by donkey team cost forty-one pounds a ton. They freighted to all points of the compass and they freighted anything of almost any weight. In particular, they were invaluable to the mines setting up far from the railheads.

The first buildings at Alice Springs (then known as Stuart), founded in 1888, were constructed of material brought from the Oodnadatta railhead by camel. A further 300 miles northwards from Alice Springs, at Tennant Creek, the mines, as late as 1929, were supplied by camels from the Oodnadatta railhead as was Newcastle Waters, 180 miles further north again.

Out to the east, Birdsville and Milparinka were supplied from Marree, the nearest station on the Central Australian Railway to Queensland. Here, considered to be one of the hottest places in Australia, Afghans comprised half the population in the early days.

Over in New South Wales, the railheads of Cobar, Bourke, and Broken Hill were the mecca for camel trains bringing in wool from the Darling River area. South Australia had sent its rail up to Broken Hill in 1887, and Bourke was connected to Sydney by rail in 1885, and Cobar in 1892.

Above: *The fettlers' gang at Oodnadatta, South Australia, 1905*

Below: *Ore train at Eleanor Reef, Pine Creek, Northern Territory, 1895*

Above: *Palmerston Railway Station (now Darwin), Northern Territory, in 1895—the station described in* We of the Never Never

Below: *Replacing sleepers that have been eaten by white ants on the North Australia Railway*

Most of the camels used in Australia were brought direct from Karachi to Port Augusta. Here in the railway town at the head of Spencer Gulf, the railway families became blasé about the sight of camel teams of up to four hundred animals lurching down their streets on the way out to Beltana in the desert-like hinterland. The cry of "Hoosh! Hoosh! Hooshta!" was as common in their street as "Gee up" in the streets of more conventional Australian towns.

Three large camel depots were set up beyond Beltana by the South Australian Government for training and depasturing camels as well as breeding. While other children learned to ride bicycles, most of the children of the railway towns in this desert area tried riding camels. Mulloorina, 300 square miles of pastoral lease, housed up to 500 camels at a time. There on the edge of Lake Eyre, the Afghans and Australian camel-men tended their herds between their wild rides to the railhead at Marree.

For nearly forty years the railhead of the Central Australian Railway was at Oodnadatta. Then the rails stretched to Alice Springs in 1929, but even before that, a greater menace to camels had passed through Oodnadatta: the first motorised road train. Brigadier Dollery who was in charge of the army operation on that path-finding trip said, "They stood there watching us come, all the camel drivers in their turbans. We were the finish for them, and they knew it."

Coming to the railheads and the stations along the track were other camel-powered contraptions. The policeman at Marree used one. He patrolled from the railhead out over the Birdsville track in a light riding buggy pulled by a camel. But the most famous—and for twenty years—was the mail buggy that met the train at Abminga Siding. This came from Andado, a station out on the Simpson Desert borderlands, and was the rear end of a T model Ford, its engine removed, and its wheels making light work of the sandhills. The explorer C. T. Madigan saw it at the siding and asked the driver how long it would take his pair of camels to cover the eighty miles from Abminga to Andado, and was told by "Fred" that he'd do it in a day of non-stop travelling. "It was a great sight to see it in action with Fred at the steering wheel."

At the top of the continent, reaching down as though it still might get to Alice Springs, is the northern end of the line that was to be the Trans-Continental.

The station at Darwin has not changed since the days when Mrs Aeneas Gunn set off south on her way to Roper River country. In her book *We of the Never Never,* she describes her trip. "We were waiting for the train that was to take us just as far as it could—150 miles—on our way to the Never-Never. It was out of town just then, up-country somewhere, billabonging in true bush-whacker style, but was expected to return in a day or two, when it would be at our service."

Then she climbed on board—there are no platforms on the line—and they were off. "From sun-up to sun-down on Tuesday, the train glided quietly forward on its way towards the Never-Never; and I experienced the kindly consideration that it always shows to travellers; it boiled a billy for us at its furnace; loitered through the pleasantest valleys; smiled indulgently, and slackened speed whenever we made merry with blacks, by pelting them with chunks of water-melon; and generally waited on us hand and foot, the Man-in-Charge pointing out the beauty spots and places of interest, and making tea for us at frequent intervals.

Above: *A lunch stop at Batchelor, Northern Territory, in 1895, when the line from Darwin ran only as far as Pine Creek.*
Below: *The "Watering Stop" near Darwin River, 1895*

Above: *The old railway jetty, Darwin, photographed in 1895. It was bombed by the Japanese in 1942.*
Below: *The elegant days of leisurely travel on the Darwin to Pine Creek line, 1895*

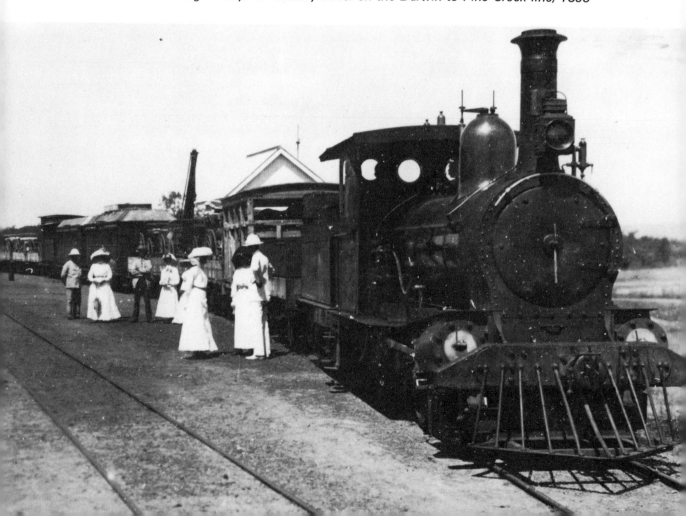

"It was a delightful train—just a simple-hearted, chivalrous, weather-beaten old bush-whacker, at the service of the entire Territory. 'There's nothing the least bit officious or standoffish about it,' I was saying, when the Man-in-Charge came in with the first billy of tea.

"'Of course not!' he said, unhooking cups from various crooked-up fingers. 'It's a Territorian, you see.' 'And had all the false veneer of civilisation peeled off long ago,' the Maluka said, adding, with a sly look at my discarded gloves and gossamer, 'It's wonderful how quietly the Territory does its work.'

"The Man-in-Charge smiled openly as he poured out the tea, proving thereby his kinship with all other Territorians; and as the train came to a standstill, swung off and slipped some letters into a box nailed to an old tree-trunk.

"At the far end of the train, away from the engine, the passengers' car had been placed, and as in front of it a long, long line of low stacked sinuous trucks slipped along in the rear of the engine, all was open view before us; and all day long, as the engine trudged onward—hands in pocket, so to speak, and whistling merrily as it trudged—I stood beside the Maluka on the little platform in front of the passengers' car, drinking in my first deep, intoxicating draught of the glories of the tropical bush.

"There were no fences to shut us in; and as the train zig-zagged through jungle and forest and river-valley—stopping now and then to drink deeply at magnificent rivers ablaze with water-lilies—it almost seemed as though it were some kindly Mammoth creature, wandering at will through the bush.

"Here and there, kangaroos and other wild creatures of the bush loped out of our way, and sitting up, looked curiously after us; again and again little groups of blacks hailed us, and scrambled after water-melon and tobacco, with shouts of delight, and, invariably, on nearing the tiny settlements along the railway, we drove before us white fleeing flocks of goats.

"At every settlement we stopped and passed the time of day and, giving out mail-bags, moved on again into the forest. Now and again, stockmen rode out of the timber and received mail-bags, and once a great burly bushman, a staunch old friend of the Maluka's, boarded the train, and greeted him with a hearty hand-shake.

"But although the Territory train does not need to bend its neck to the galling yoke of a minute timetable, yet, like all bush-whackers, it prefers to strike its supper camp before night-fall, and after allowing us a good ten minutes' chat, it blew a deferential 'Ahem' from its engine, as a hint that it would like to be 'getting along.' The bushman took the hint, and after a hearty 'Good luck, missus!' and a 'chin, chin old man,' left us.

"Until sundown we jogged quietly on, meandering through further pleasant places and meetings; drinking tea and chatting with the Man-in-Charge between whiles, extracting a maximum of pleasure from a minimum rate of speed: for travelling in the Territory has not yet passed that ideal stage where the travelling itself—the actual going—is all pleasantness."

T. Southwell Keely, a traveller early this century, wasn't quite so gallant about the train, but then he wasn't on his honeymoon. "The discomfits of railway travel in the north, of which one has received so many warnings, become apparent. It is a sweltering hot day. Despite the recent rains, clouds of dust are swept up and surge through the passenger compartments. If you leave the windows open, grass seeds and gravel and coal dust are hurled through the length of the compartment in thick choking waves. Passengers disagree with opening or closing the windows. The alternatives are to choke with blinding, cutting grass seeds, or to suffocate in a sweltering vacuum. Piles of dust and grass seeds gambol on the floor and accumulate on the khaki-covered seats. You walk unsteadily along the swaying train to the platform where a water-bag is swinging precariously. The water tastes of coal dust and grass seeds and gravel.

"The train pulls up at Darwin River for water and the engine-driver obligingly waits while you take a photograph. He will whistle when he is ready to move on and will give you ample warning. The main road from Darwin to Adelaide breasts the line, but you have difficulty in finding it, for it is overgrown with willowy grass ten feet high. A few feet away and the train is hidden behind a bulwark of grass, and only a thin spiral of steam betrays its presence. The engine rattles across the Darwin River swollen by rains to a magnificent stream. The heavy jungle fringes the bank, and struggling palms grope upwards through the undergrowth. The noise of the train sends a crocodile scuttling into the river.

"Rum Jungle is the next stopping place. The name of the station is almost illegible through the tangled green grass which surrounds the siding. It earned the quaint name as a consequence of the notorious activities of teamsters in the old days who occasionally broached their freight at this old meeting place. Two or three rambling corrugated iron buildings and a few vegetable gardens, whose owners are hard put to it to beat back the encroaching grass, comprise the settlement. They all gather around the train to hear the latest Darwin gossip and to collect their parcels. The Wet season has made the main road impassable, and it is this big day of the week when the train arrives, for they have no other means of communication with the outside world during the monsoonal period.

"The drab dust-ridden train rattles on through the same unvarying type of country, with its scattered eucalyptus, bauhinia, bloodwood, boxwood, stringybark and cabbage-top trees, and pulls up at a tiny station known as Batchelor. Numerous strange stories are told about Government attempts in the early days to establish experimental farms in the rich flats surrounding the settlement. Huge consignments of seeds were sent to Darwin. An enthusiastic Government servant decided to prevent dust getting into the seeds before they reached the farm, and so emptied them all into a corrugated iron tank. The farmers did not know whether they were sowing cyprus pine or cucumbers.

"No habitation breaks the landscape from Batchelor to Grove Hill, and this depressing lack of any sign of development continues between stations for practically the entire length of the line. At Grove Hill there are a few struggling vegetable gardens, then the puffing train passes again into the inevitable bush, past the lonely graves of two unidentified pioneers, and pulls up to a groaning stop at Adelaide River. The township comprises the Railway Hotel, alongside the line. The settlement could not muster a dozen whites. A pastoralist walks up to the engine and thanks the driver. It appears that a few weeks previously his motor car had bogged near the railway

Above: Ganger Tom Flynn and his wife Nellie, who were used as characters in Xavier Herbert's Capricornia, *at Adelaide River, Northern Territory.*
Below: Pioneers of the Daly River area ready to head west from the Adelaide River siding in 1895

line. He waited for the train to pass and the driver stopped to see if he could assist. A rope was tied to the car and the train dragged it clear.

"The protesting engine lumbers out of Adelaide River, and the train enters the metalliferous country which it traverses throughout the rest of the day until the stopping place at Pine Creek is reached. On either side of the rails alluvial miners have scratched and scarred the surface and riddled the hills with holes. Once there were nearly three thousand Chinese miners scattered around Brock Creek. Hundreds of thousands of pounds worth of mining machinery is lying corroding in the surrounding hills in the abandoned holdings. A branch tram line used to run eighteen miles into the hills when the diggings were being worked. When the holding was abandoned the line was pulled up, and upon reaching the terminus it was found that the tram had been forgotten. The line had then to be replaced to get the expensive tram back to the railway line. Then the line was pulled up again.

"A few of the remaining prospectors gather round the tin hut which comprises the siding, ironically named Fountain Head—the nearest water is at least four miles away. Pine Creek, the terminus of the railway, lives on the memories of the glories of the past. When the line was constructed it was a prosperous mining centre."

Of all States, South Australia was the most courageous in the building of railways, first their little horse-drawn Goolwa line to draw the wool from western New South Wales, then the line to the border to take south to the smelters' hungry mouth the ore from Broken Hill, and then, the great plan for a line from Adelaide to Darwin, 1,900 miles.

While the line crept up from the southern end, contractors began work at "The Top End," from Darwin. The first section, from Darwin to Adelaide River, was opened in June 1888. It reached the mining settlement of Pine Creek in October 1889, Emungalen in May 1917, Mataranka (near the old Elsey Homestead on the Roper River) in July 1928, and stopped, perhaps for all time, at Birdum in September 1929.

The first section, built by the South Australian Government Railways, was the only section of railway in Australia to use Chinese labour. These men, upwards of 3,000, including 2,124 who arrived in the one year, 1887, were brought out by the contractors with no obligation to return them to their own country. Most stayed on and became the founders of the Darwin Chinese community, today a large and important part of the Darwin population.

The Commonwealth assumed control of the Northern Australia Railway in 1911 in accordance with the 1907 "Northern Territory Surrender Act" and the 1910 "Northern Territory Acceptance Act."

The Commonwealth had assumed control of the Port Augusta to Oodnadatta section in 1907—the Act of Parliament providing for the contribution by the Commonwealth of a Trans-Continental Railway from South Australia—but without a completion date being given. At that time, South Australia had completed 688 miles of railway from Adelaide to Oodnadatta, and 146 miles from Darwin to Pine Creek— 834 miles of the distance of 1,900 miles between the southern capital and Darwin.

When the southern line was later brought up to Alice Springs and the northern line brought south to Birdum, a gap of 603 miles was left. And so it remains.

There's been a lot of laughter, a lot of drama on both ends of the lost line, and much heartache. Len Scott, one of the old guards on the Northern line once said, "There were our cattle trucks of lepers we'd cart off up to the leprosarium out in the bay off Darwin; there were settlers battling to make a go of it and being brought in to have a baby, or see a doctor with a snake-bite; there were the toughest men always playing jokes—it was a whole life down that line that told you more about the Territory than you ever heard or read about."

A passenger waiting for the train at Batchelor, Northern Territory, in 1895

The busy Quorn locomotive depot in the days when the town was the hub of northern South Australia lines

FOR WANT OF THE LONESOME WHISTLE

LOTTIE AND JOE PICKFORD live on in the town that was left to mark time with no hope of the trumpet of Reveille to breathe life into it again. Lottie is a woman who challenged the Prime Minister of England; and her husband Joe formed an orchestra in the desert with a kangaroo skin for drum. They are part of a galaxy of the toughest, bravest men and women the Australian inland has produced.

Why were they left behind? Why has the bustle and vitality gone from their town? An old camel driver friend of Joe knows: "For want of the banshee wail of a train whistle," he says. "You'd hear it coming over the prairie out here, and it was like fresh reinforcements being brought up to keep the town going."

Quorn, South Australia, was a railway town. Suddenly the trains stopped coming. Lively young people left, and all that remained was the pride of the old ones.

Here you see what happens to a town when the last train whistle blows, when the lonesome wail from an engine fades across the plains with an ache that stirs only memories and cannot kindle hope. They have a big hotel called the "Transcontinental," built when they thought the railways from Perth to Sydney and Darwin to Adelaide would pass this way; another called "The Grand Junction." There remains a solid railway station, railway buildings, train crew quarters, and more old railmen per head of population than any place in Australia. "That's all we've got. We're lucky if we see a train a week," Harold Willard, the camel driver speaks up. "Quorn.is a railway ghost town, its zest stripped from it when it was at its peak."

There's not a soldier, sailor, or airman who went north to Alice Springs and Darwin during the war years who doesn't know Quorn. The railways came up from Adelaide, across from Perth and down from Broken Hill and Sydney, the troop trains rolled over thousands of miles of desert country and pulled up for re-coaling and watering at Quorn.

"Everybody out for the best feed this side of the Black Stump," the Transport Officers would call, and the lads leapt down onto the dusty platform and sat down at a meal, there on the edge of no-where—and agreed with the Officers. Many of the women working on this voluntary effort were railway widows, women whose husbands were away as train crew, bringing their weary load home through the blackout. "We often got in dead-beat," Joe Pickford, the old ganger recalls, "and the missus would be onto us, to cut wood for her copper. 'There's a train due' and off you'd go to get her puddings or meats or whatever was cooking to boil in the copper out in the yard."

Harold Willard, "Spider," the old camel driver, was in charge of the big barracks for train crews during the war years. "Every woman in Quorn should have been given a medal for their war effort. Think of it, out here on the edge of the desert; no refrigerators, no electric stoves or gas, no great homesteads to set the work out in." (The women were in fact honoured by the Queen, who decorated the President of the local C.W.A. as recognition of the work done by the women of this little town on the edge of the desert.)

They were bustling days. But Quorn had been bustling since it first began. In the old days of steam, the crews were changed there and the engines coaled and watered. As well as the work that this made for men of the town, the surrounding cattle stations called for their weekly supplies and mail. And so the shopping centre grew. Big, many-bedroomed hotels were built and substantial businesses, including a three storied flour mill, flourished. "We knew Quorn would stand for as long as the railway went through, and seeing that Quorn was on the way to everywhere, we never dreamed that the railways would leave us."

"It wasn't until well after the war that rumours first began to filter up here on the prairie. The line to Alice Springs was being re-aligned, and they said it might by-pass us. Sure enough, it did. But we weren't desperate. The building had started on the new standard gauge from Perth to Sydney. It would *have* to come through. But it didn't. It too by-passed our railway town."

So now, miles from anywhere, with the dust of the desert often rolling in a thick cloud over their houses, what do these tough men and women of another era do?

Charlotte Pickford knows. "There was nothing more we could do about the railway. All the deputations, protests and letters in the world couldn't bring the railway through Quorn again. And once the railway goes, these little towns are done for. Unless the people pull together and hold it up by the boot straps. That's just what they're doing in Quorn. Life goes on even though there is nothing to keep the young people in the town.

"We've got good hostels started for pioneers, men and women; we can work for these; there's the old mill that's a tourist attraction; there's the C.W.A. and church groups, and we still cater whenever we can. This last University vacation about 250 young people from all States came to Quorn for singing. Choral groups from Universities. But mainly we yarn about old times, that's what we do."

Charlotte and her husband Joe are as typical as railways in these parts ever gathered, inasmuch as they were battlers of the type that made this word almost revered in the Australia of the Depression years.

They came here in the 1930s from Wales, where the times were so bad they thought anywhere else must be better. Charlotte got their fare to Australia by accident. She wrote a letter to the Prime Minister of England. And she didn't pull her punches. She was incensed that the Prince of Wales (the late Duke of Windsor) had been rebuked by Parliament for having called for help for the Welsh people. "He had been into the cottages where there was no food, no money, no hope, where a woman was having a baby and no blanket to cover her; he saw it all and he was crying with us. So I wrote and told Stanley Baldwin what I had seen. And I finished my letter by saying that I wouldn't stay in this country. I wrote, 'I will not bring up my sons in a land where honest work is denied them, where they have watched their father, for three years, plod from mine to mine in the Welsh valleys begging for work. And not getting it. Somewhere in the world there must be a place where good men are permitted to work.'"

Charlotte received a formal reply, but, with a note added by the Prime Minister himself, that her description of the plight of people in the Welsh valleys moved him.

Above: *Great hotels stand almost empty in Quorn, South Australia, "for want of the lonesome whistle."*
Below: *The residents of Quorn have refurbished this old mill (right) to attract tourists*

"Then, one day, out of the blue, two women turned up in our town and asked for me. They had been at a meeting of women in London and the Prime Minister's wife had read my letter out aloud. These women now came to offer to help me and mine get out. They bought us suitcases and gave us enough money for food and the fare to Australia. I had a brother in South Australia, so we came here. And found there were men looking for work ahead of us. But then we got a break. There was a terrible downpour of rain that Christmas and by New Year they were calling for men to go to the washaways on the Alice Springs line. They said to bring old clothes, that it would be work in water to the waist, for nine hours a day. So off Joe went with his mining boots and underground gear, all he had, and when he came home three weeks later, he presented me with a five pound note, the first I'd seen."

He spent the next twelve months with only an odd day's work. Then he chanced a job in a railway gang, and went 600 miles up the line. "It's a hard country you've come to," the ganger told him. "It's a hard country I've come from," answered Joe. The next thing the ganger said was, "I suppose you could do with a bit of a feed, boy." And Joe had a better meal than he'd had for twelve months.

It was here, at Abminga, that the navvies formed a band; one man on the swannee whistle, another with an accordion, the cook with violin, and Joe with a drum he made by stretching a kangaroo skin over a wooden frame. The lack of women didn't stop them from having a dance. "Five women would come from the cattle stations out on the plains. Their menfolk and us navvies would sleep on the verandah and the women and children would have our bunks. They'd come on Friday to meet the train and we'd have scrubbed our kitchen out and put the tables into the pantry. Us 'musicians' sat on the tables and the floor was cleared for dancing. We made a tennis court with picks and shovels and played tennis the next morning, mixed doubles, everything!"

When a vacancy in a permanent gang came up Joe wired to Charlotte. "Boat sails Thursday. All aboard." And so she and the children arrived on "The Ghan," the train to Alice Springs, and they in their turn became organisers of social life around the railway settlements of Oodnadatta, Marree, and Quorn.

In those days "Spider" Willard was "riding the desert schooner" at the big camel camps, coming in to meet the trains, loading up his kneeling animals, then, "Hoosh! Hoosh! Hooshta!" getting them on their feet and heading out to the cattle stations over the rim of the horizon. He insists that most of these trips were quite short. Now in his eighties, he says, "A few hundred miles at the most." A matter of weeks only. "What was a long trip? There was that time in 1926 when I left with a surveyor and seven camels and didn't get back for two and a half years." In that time he and the other man had beaten off an attack by Aborigines in the Musgrave Ranges, and survived an even worse battle against thirst in the waterless barren wastes. "In all that time I never saw a fence or a road and didn't sleep under an iron roof."

Ringers, shearers, cocky-farmers, and navvies came to these railway towns. Women, who worked harder and faced greater danger than their city cousins dreamt of, kept homes together in the dusty wilderness, and carved out a gay, full life for their families.

They bring out their mementoes—not many, for they had lived spartan lives. But they were the only proof they now had, perhaps even to themselves. To talk railways to them is to become a part of their lives. "Spider" has sent the author a Christmas card ever since she first met him. The first one was a picture of Santa Claus with the words, "I hope I find you in my Christmas Stocking," and underneath this, in his own spidery handwriting, "Spider" had written, "Yours respectfully, Spider Willard."

These are just three of the people stranded when the railways left the town high and dry. The town is a treasury of men and women with a story that takes you on a walk through a legendary past of the never-never land of Australia.

They have all gathered in Quorn, the town that served the desert area, an exciting, alert centre when they moved there. "Some women crave to get down to the city," Charlotte Pickford says. "I was always happy to get to Quorn," And now the long, lonesome whistle is rarely heard in the town that it shunted into prosperity and then forgot about.

Joe Pickford, "Spider" Willard, and Charlotte Pickford—three who stayed on in Quorn, South Australia, when the railways left the town behind

A steam train can ease through flood waters up to the footplate, but a diesel cannot tolerate over four inches of water over the line. Some steam locomotives have been retained for such emergencies on the Central Australia Railway

AWAY WITH THE FLYING GANG

The·Flying Gang

I served my time, in the days gone by,
 In the railway's clash and clang,
And I worked my way to the end, and I
 Was the head of the "Flying Gang."
'Twas a chosen band that was kept at hand
 In case of an urgent need;
Was it south or north, we were started forth
 And away at our utmost speed,
If word reached town that a bridge was down,
 The imperious summons rang—
"Come out with the pilot engine sharp,
 And away with the flying gang."

Then a piercing scream and a rush of steam
 As the engine moved ahead;
With measured beat by the slum and street
 Of the busy town we fled,
By the uplands bright and the homesteads white
 With the rush of the western gale—
And the pilot swayed with the pace we made
 As she rocked on the ringing rail.
And the country children clapped their hands
 As the engine's echoes rang,
But their elders said: "There is work ahead
 When they send for the flying gang."

Then across the miles of the saltbush plains
 That gleamed with the morning dew,
Where the grasses waved like the ripening grain
 The pilot engine flew—
A fiery rush in the open bush
 Where the grade marks seemed to fly,
And the order sped on the wires ahead,
 The pilot must go by.
The Governor's special must stand aside,
 And the fast express go hang;
Let your orders be that the line is free
 For the boys of the flying gang.

A. B. Paterson

It's out with the pilot engine fast, and away with the "flying gang" when natural disasters hit the tracks. There is scarcely a railman outside the cities, who hasn't been called out for flood, fire, or heat buckling the rails. As old Joe Pickford, the ganger on the line to Alice Springs recalls, his first job in the depression was to go north to a washaway. "You'll be up to your waist in water all day," a bystander said as the pilot train left Marree station. "He was wrong," Joe says. "We were up to our armpits."

That line floods still, and will do so for as long as it runs on that route. The 539 miles of line from Marree to Alice Springs is a narrow three and a half foot gauge railway built across a spiderweb of watercourses flowing south-east to Lake Eyre. Literally hundreds of river beds are crossed. Normally dry until an inch or two of rain falls in the catchment areas, the watercourses then become vast inland lakes of swirling muddy water.

While death by thirst has overtaken many an unfortunate traveller in Australia's traditionally dry Centre, there is nothing unusual in a number of these large watercourses flooding each year. The Finke River flooded four times in 1968, and the Alberga came down on a two-mile front carrying everything before it, including the trestle bridge. Even smaller river beds, such as the Temple Bar, a few miles south of Alice Springs, can bring down enough water to leave the railway line suspended in the air.

When the water is higher than the rails, the trains must wait until the floodwaters have receded. (A diesel engine can only wade through water no more than three

Above: *A spectacular washaway on the line at Dog Trap Gully, Victoria, in 1891.*
Facing page: *A pig-sty of sleepers built by fettlers to keep the line open until permanent repairs can be carried out—York to Bruce Rock line, Western Australia, 1955.*
Below: *Washaway at bridge over Avon River, Bushy Park, Victoria, in 1893*

inches above the rails.) The waiting may halt train services for several hours to a week, or more.

On the Central Australia line at one washaway in 1929, they put in pig-stys for nearly a hundred miles down as far as Bundoomah. "On the way back up to Alice Springs to get the train out, we had to build the b . . . . . pig-stys again: the floods had come down again and swept them away." That was Driver George Williams talking. "The navvies had to struggle down stream and collect the sleepers and set them up again." It took five months for the line to be rebuilt.

The pig-stys referred to are the permanent-way men's method of temporarily bolstering up a bridge or culvert where the piers have been washed away. Sleepers are criss-crossed from the ground up to the height of the original track and the temporary line built over this.

In 1938, at Margaret Siding, 3,000 new sleepers and 300 old ones were used to get the trains moving after the waters came down. Passengers on a train trapped by the waters had an experience they will dine out on for the rest of their lives. "Barbecues and sing-songs every night," they said. "Log fires—and, out on the prairie, the gangs

The Flying Gang using rocks in an attempt to fill a small washaway caused by a sudden summer storm in northern South Australia

that were brought from north and south were slaving away through the night."

In contrast to the Territory, Gippsland, Victoria, is green, wet, and lush, and yet it has few floods of the magnitude of the Centre. An exception that devastated the railways was the great floods of 1934. On the last days of November, the rain fell ceaselessly. The drains, taking the water out to sea from the Kooweerup Swamps area, were running a banker. Then came disaster in the form of a spring tide. The flood waters rolling down the canals were halted by the banked-up outlets and the yellow-brown water washed the canal banks away and rolled in over the land.

A locomotive swept off the line during 1932 floods on the Alice Springs to Quorn line

One of the early railway accidents in Australia, at Parramatta Station, 1879

RAILWAY SPINE

THERE WERE STORIES told of the dangers of travelling by train in the early days. A poem on this theme appeared in the magazine of the Victorian Railways as follows:

A haughty young damsel named Maud Mary Mack,
Tried to alight next the opposite track,
The train being crowded the guard could not see
Now Maud's got a tombstone to her memory.

There had been such solemn warnings from Mother England on the dangers of railroad travel that antipodeans could scarcely have been unaware of the outcome of a prolonged debauch in riding the rail. There was the story about the addling of the brain of business men by the velocity of the journey from Manchester to London. "They often forgot what they went for, and had to write home to find out." One elderly gentleman "became so impregnated with velocity that he dashed headlong into an iron post and shivered it to pieces."

These stories came to Australia with the new settlers, becoming part of the lore of the new land; they were embellished through time, and influenced by local geography, they increased in number, variety, and raciness.

In 1866 a solemn warning was issued by Dr J. E. Erickson, surgeon, on what he termed "Railway Spine." A person usually developed this, he said, while "quite unconscious that any serious accident has happened. He feels that he has been violently jolted and shaken, perhaps somewhat giddy and confused but no bones broken." But the symptoms soon appear. "He has lost bodily energy, mental capacity, business aptitude, looks worn and ill, becomes irritable and easily fatigued. The memory is defective, the thoughts confused, the temper changed for the worse . . . ." Many more, mostly awful, changes occur. "The gait is remarkable and characteristic. He walks unsteadily, keeping his feet somewhat apart, spine, head erect. He has a sensation as of a cord tied around the waist.

"The condition of the genitourinary organs is seldom much deranged in the cases under consideration, as there is usually no paralysis of the sphincters. Neither retention of urine nor incontinence of flatus and faeces occur. Sometimes . . . irritability of the bladder is a prominent symptom. The urine generally retains acidity, sometimes markedly, at others but very slightly so. As there is no retention, it does not become alkaline, ammoniacal, or otherwise offensive.

"The sexual desire and power are usually greatly impaired and often entirely lost. Not invariably so, however. The wife of Case 5 miscarried twice during the twelve months succeeding her husband's accident. I have never heard priapism complained of."

The surgeon gives little hope of a cure for the disease of his time, saying that there has never been a case of complete restoration to health from "railway spine."

The very nature of its motive force causes railway accidents to be of a dramatic nature, but the reporting of some of those in earlier years was marked by sensationalism. An article in the *Australasian Sketcher* of 1879 was entitled "Serious Railway

Above: *Someone left the swing bridge open on 22 July 1886 at Bridgewater Junction, Tasmania, and this locomotive fell through the gap.*
Below: *This engine left the line at Coal Mine Bend, Tasmania, 24 April 1877, due to a defective rail, but there were no fatalities*

Accident at Parramatta," and is worth quoting: "The first serious case of 'telescoping' in connection with the railway system of the colony took place at Parramatta yesterday afternoon, and it is almost miraculous that it was not attended with fatal consequences. It is the most serious accident of the kind that has transpired since the terrible Emu Plains disaster of some 18 months ago, by which two men were killed and others were injured.

"Yesterday, being Boxing Day several thousands of people proceeded by railway to the Parramatta and Hawkesbury Races, inspired with confidence in the good management of the railways, and little dreaming of the terrible shock their nervous systems were to experience. The races in both places were over, and the Sydney people who had proceeded to the Hawkesbury and Parramatta meetings were preparing to return home. A large number of those at Windsor left in a first-class special train about five o'clock and had proceeded merrily on their way as far as Parramatta, when the engine to which their train was attached ran into a train that was stationary there and about to proceed to Sydney.

"Several hundreds of men, women and children were standing on the platform and witnessed the accident, and the excitement amongst them was intense. A number of persons had taken seats in the last two carriages of the Sydney train when the train from Windsor was observed approaching the station. It was seen by Mr Richardson, line inspector, that it had far too much way on, and that gentleman told those who were in the carriages to jump out for their lives. A large number did so, but several persons were prevented from following the injunction in consequence of the excitement and crush. The danger they were in was apparent to everyone on the platform, for the Windsor engine was crushing its way into the carriages, and making the position of the inmates' more perilous every second, and their escape almost impossible. Their shrieks were terrific, and the excitement on the platform became intensified in consequence. Women screamed and fainted and went into wild hysterics, while the hearts of men stood still with horror as they saw that it was impossible to render any assistance to those who were imprisoned in the carriages.

"At last the engine stopped its cruel progress, and instantly dozens of willing hands were ready to assist those who, it was evident, must have been seriously if not fatally injured, but in consequence of the crush and general excitement, it was impossible for several minutes to do anything in the shape of relief. In the meantime the passengers by the Windsor train had each received a shock from the concussion, which as one passenger said 'jumbled them together,' and put them into a great state of apprehension as to what had occurred. They could hear the screams of women and see men on the platform rushing to and fro, and the excitement became contagious, extending especially to ladies, whose trepidation unnerved and placed them in a fainting condition.

"Some of the men leapt from the train with a view to lending aid, for they could see at a glance that something serious had occurred. Amongst the foremost were Mr Carlisle, traffic manager—who was on the engine—Mr Evans, superintendent, and Mr John Thompson, each of whom lent invaluable aid in removing the debris of the Sydney train carriages, and those who were involved in it. These gentlemen and some constables and railway officials belonging to the place succeeded eventually in extricating about a dozen persons, and placing them in positions of safety. Then the extent and nature of the injuries were approximated, and it was ascertained that a number of those who were injured were women. Several men had nasty gashes on their faces, and one or two were bleeding profusely.

"All were in a helpless condition as a matter of course, and vehicles were procured at once with the view of sending them all to the Parramatta Infirmary. The friends of some of those who were least injured objected to this being done, but after the whole had been inspected by Dr Bottrell and Dr West, two women and three men were taken to that institution, where they were received and attended to by Dr Johnson and Dr Rutter. Those who stayed behind received all the attention it was possible to bestow on them but were nearly overrun by the crowd, who were anxious to ascertain whether anyone was killed. Joseph Murphy, a young labourer who lived at Enmore and who was conveyed to the infirmary, was the most seriously injured. He was suffering from a frightfully jagged wound in the stomach, and his groans in the infirmary were piteous."

All the states of Australia have grievously recorded their worst accidents and little Tasmania for years particularly remembered their tragedy at Campania, twenty-nine miles from Hobart on 15 February 1916. It was in the war years. "There were boys in khaki on the injured list."

The huge Garrett engine had failed to take Horseshoe Bend, the leading bogies of the rear engine left the rails and the locomotive followed, left the track, churned a way through the soft soil and rolled over, with its funnel buried deep. The newspapers of the island told the story. "An accident involving the loss of four lives and serious injury (three more died later) to a number of passengers, happened to the Launceston-Hobart express just outside Campania on Tuesday afternoon. The accident is considered the worst in Tasmanian history. There were 200 passengers on the train which left the rails two miles north of Campania, and twenty-nine miles from Hobart. Numerous men in khaki were aboard.

"The train had just negotiated the well-known Horseshoe Bend, when the passengers bumped from their seats from some violent cause. Other passengers were smiling at the discomfiture of their unseated travelling companions when a second and more violent bump warned all that a serious mishap was pending. The ugly fact was soon revealed that the engine had left the rails, and had turned completely over. The huge Garrett engine, once having left the track, had ploughed its way through the soft earth at the side of the embankment, and reaching the foot had kicked back as it were, mangling, as it did so the passengers of the oncoming carriages. The locomotive turned completely over. It now lies with its smoke funnel firmly buried in the soil. One carriage followed the same direction as the engine—to the right—and was smashed to matchwood. The cries of the injured were dreadful. The second carriage went in an opposite direction—to the left-hand side—and it was followed by all the others leaving the rails. The first and second carriages were reduced to matchwood.

"The engine driver (Philip Goodchild of Invermay) was severely hurt when the engine left the rails. With great difficulty he found his way to the steam lever, and

Above: *An unusual angle for B class locomotive No. 110 at Seymour, Victoria, 13 April 1904.*
Below: *An EE class locomotive, derailed at Ringwood, Victoria, in the early 1900s*

by his brave self sacrifice and devotion to duty prevented an explosion taking place. He was rescued from his awful predicament, but his whole body was blistered and scalded, and the skin came off in flakes.

"All those who knew anything about it were most loud in their praise of the splendid conduct of the driver. On being rescued he bore his agony with wonderful fortitude, every moment enquiring anxiously of the passengers, especially the women. When the doctor arrived he urged him almost in tears to leave him and attend to the passengers." A few hours later he died of his injuries.

"Driver Goodchild . . . sought to minimise the risk of explosion, fire, and scalding of the disabled, pinned down victims. Forgetting his personal welfare, he persevered in his efforts, and was successful, but at what a cost! What remained of this noble servant of the public was, after some time had elapsed, extricated from the debris. Driver Goodchild was literally boiled alive, only a few inches square surface on his back being left with skin. The remaining colour of the hero was a bright claret. His head, face, neck, hands, and entire body, with the exception of the small portion referred to, were completely scalded. His agony must have been dreadful. The rescue party heard the noble words, 'Let me go, lads, Oh my God! my poor passengers.' As the devoted, admiring, and most affected rescuers attempted to lift Goodchild, his skin was felt to come away from his body, with a sickening effect on the workers. That little woman from the gate-house . . . furnished a sheet upon which the stricken hero was tenderly placed.

"Driver Goodchild died this morning. Thus died a proved martyr to the call of duty. He truly gave his life for his passengers."

Next day the driver's body was brought home by train to Launceston and the funeral left the railway station, with the coffin "borne from the train to the hearse on the shoulders of four of the deceased's former comrades, Drivers Hay, Connors, Best, and Wise." Headed by the Railway Band playing the "Dead March," the procession moved off. Hundreds of spectators gathered paying their last respects to "a man whose noble act of self sacrifice had stirred all hearts."

★   ★   ★   ★

And of course the poets did not lag behind the prose-writers in writing about the excitement and hazards of travelling on the trains and the dedication of the men who ran them. One such poem describes the crash of the Temora train. It was written by Mrs M. E. Poole of Stockingbingal, and appeared in the *Albury Banner and Wodonga Express* on 25 October 1929.

THE ILL-FATED TEMORA TRAIN

Out from Sydney Central station,
  On its fatal journey back,
The Temora Mail came steaming,
  Down a foggy midnight track.

And its whistles brought the echoes
  From the ranges near at hand,
As that fast up-country mail train
  Raced athwart the Southern land.

Above: *The boiler blew up on this G1 locomotive at Zeehan, Tasmania, on 27 May 1899. Both the driver and fireman were killed.*
Below: *This mishap took place on 27 May 1914 at Paringa, South Australia. Horses were used to clear the line*

"Safety First?" A 1920 Victorian publicity picture in Keystone-Cops style, part of an attempt to cut the growing accident rate

Ever onward through the stations,
　　Right away and past Moss Vale
Came a streak of carriage lights
　　On that fast Temora Mail.

And the roaring of the engine
　　Through the country could be heard
Till at last it came to Exeter
　　Where the fatal smash occurred.

And it happened that the signals
　　Were obscured that foggy night.
Or the accident in question,
　　Would no doubt been something light.

So the driver of the mail train
　　Got no timely warning sign,
Till the flying train collided,
　　With a goods train on the line.

What a scene for one to witness,
　　Dead and dying everywhere.
While the cries of wounded people
　　Floated sadly on the air.

From beneath the awful wreckage,
　　Where so many souls were slain,
At few seconds notice
　　On that ill-fated train.

Broken cars and wounded people,
　　Dying souls and many dead,
From the badly damaged guard's van
　　To the engine up ahead.

Could be heard that night at Exeter,
　　'Mid the cries and groans of pain,
That were uttered by the people,
　　Who would never rise again.

Parting words of love and friendship
  Left for someone to convey,
To the dying one's relations
  Who are many miles away.

Tell my people when you see them
  Not to worry when I'm gone
For I've prayed that God will help them
  And I'm going further on.

And just say "'Twas so sudden,"
  Just a crash and here we are,
Dying, wounded, sick and bleeding,
  Near a smashed-up railway car.

Mind and don't forget to tell them,
  All the things I have said.
That is all. Goodbye, remember,
  And another one is dead.

Such a wreck as this will linger,
  In the hearts of men for aye,
And especially those who witnessed,
  How their comrades passed away.

But I'm sure the chosen people,
  Who have gone beyond recall,
Will be happy with each other
  In the best land after all.

Wait awhile heart-broken people,
  Wait awhile 'mid grief and strife,
For that Great Eternal Mail Train
  Just across the bridge of life.

You may mourn the loss of loved ones
  But the loved ones will not fail,
To be there when you are coming,
  On that Great Eternal Mail.

An accident on the South Australian Railways on 13 April 1865, from an original sketch at the scene by D. D. Daley

Top: *Ploughing by camel team during construction of the Trans-Australia Railway.*
Bottom: *The Indian-Pacific speeds across the 2,461-mile standard gauge line from Sydney to Perth, February 1970*

THE LONG STRAIGHT

IT USED TO BE PART of the talk of railway lovers to link the "Trans" with the "Ghan" and the "Darwin Line" in affectionate chiakking. The coming into the field of the glamour train the "Indian-Pacific" has put the across-Australia run into world class and ousted the romance—and incidentally, the dust, heat, and discomfort, *and,* some will say, the fun.

The "Peaceful-Redman," as the navvies call the "Indian-Pacific," is, as advertised, a mobile luxury hotel, and passengers, travelling in such a way that their clothes are as clean when they finish the journey as when they start are not likely to appreciate the enjoyment old timers speak of when "getting off the train absolutely covered in soot."

Almost up to the coming of diesels, the "Trans" was a homely train, a country thing—a desert country thing at that. It traversed 1,051 miles of desert land, it crossed no stream of water, and ran over the Nullarbor Plain, named because of its treelessness. On it is a stretch of nearly 300 miles of track without a curve, "The Long Straight," the longest such in the world.

With experienced drivers, many of whom lived beside the track, such a trip could never be dull. There were stops to pick wildflowers, stops to look at the fettlers' pets of dingo pups and white cave owls brought up from the limestone caves that riddle the plain.

There were the Aborigines besieging the train at Ooldea where Daisy Bates had her camp; the train carried men who only recently stepped out from the land that no white man had trod. There were the navvies calling out, "Paper! Paaaaper!"

Today if a navvy called out "Paper," the traveller could only shake his head and murmur, "Sorry mate, can't get the window open." An air-conditioned luxury train is only as much fun as the people on it; it can never, in old-timers' minds, take the place of the bush-whacking old "Trans."

If times have changed dramatically for passengers, there has been little change in atmosphere for the railmen here. It is still a land apart, different from any other, a region to love or to loathe. It is still an arena where men are forced to find what reserves they have or have not.

To the railmen who are involved on either end of this long rail these settlers are special. Jim Averies, Manager of the Provisions Store at Port Augusta is a good example. "They're out there, cut off from what the rest of us know as 'the world,' their life is so different we can scarcely comprehend the division between us and them. Life is involved closely with necessities out there. The non-arrival of something ordered, or the wrong brand, can be a gigantic thing in their realm. They look on the coming of the "Tea and Sugar," as they call the provision train, as a tremendous break in the sameness of their days. They wait to unpack their goods, to gasp with pleasure at things most of us no longer notice, and fly off the handle if they consider there is any change from what they asked for. Sometimes they write rude, angry letters to me. I never ignore them. I carefully investigate and then write to them explaining—if we were wrong apologising, if not, politely telling the truth, and,

Above: *The track layer at the South Australian border, 29 August 1916, Trans-Australia Railway.*

Centre: *The Trans-Australia line would not have been built without the aid of camel transport.*

Below: *The rails are joined in the presence of a large crowd of workers on 17 October 1917, Trans-Australia Railway*

always, wishing them well. I was a railway boy, all my family were. I know what these things mean."

A sample of letters Jim has received in the past few years illustrate his comments:

Port Pirie

Dear Sir,
I am writing to ask would I be able to have XOS frock not tight fitting but one on the waist band suitable for a wedding not a dear one or no frock send 5 yards of material no woollen or crimplene no green or brown also 1 electric jug and cord no frock could I have the material down for Thursday so I can get it made up for Saturday cannot have if on special account so not send them

Yours trst

— — — — —

A Note: Please send 4 lb of 3 cornered pumpkin.

The long straight—nearly 300 miles without bend or rise—across the Nullarbor Plain on the Trans-Australia Railway

Above: *The "Tea and Sugar" train has arrived at a lonely siding on the Trans-Australia Railway.*
Below: *These semi-trailer drivers have loaded their trucks on the piggy-back service from Kalgoorlie to Port Augusta*

Cook

Sir,

Find enclosed measure for ring this is exact all by being round I would like ladys wedding ring as discussed on phone 1 flat wide plain ring (gold) price range about 10–15 dollars could I possibly get this as soon as possible as my wife is having a baby very soon and she lost her other one.

Thanking you,
— — — — —

P.S. Could this be put on Special if not current account.

Thank you

(Note: Beneath this was taped a round plastic bottle top for size.)

Immarna

Dear Mr Avis,

Do you think I could if possible if I could get a 22 single shot rifle on a special account please because a rifle comes in handy up these parts please

— — — — —

P.S. on account of dingoes.

our house is 457
Watson

Dear Father Christmas

How are you? If you are good will you bring us some presents please. Paulle is 4 and he would like a train with a key in it. Samantha is 2 and she wants a box of Big Blocks Leah is 9 months could she have a Pink Teddy. I am 6 could I have a mouse trap game. If you havent got these we will have a surprise. I hope your Reindeers are well.

Love from Linda, Paulie, Samantha, and Leah

Probably, to a passenger today, these men—and women—are the most colourful things left of the line. Leaping and cavorting like wild colonial boys of another era, they cross behind the express as it goes by to get to the "Tea and Sugar" pulled into the siding. "The b—'s are probably getting stuck into turkey and plum pud," they say to the roving butcher in his van.

They have not changed. They are chips off the old blocks who came out here and built the line with camels and horsedrawn scoops between 1912 and 1917. Some of the stories they tell of one another could be swapped for stories told of those legendary men who were here half a century ago.

"We mightn't have much money, but we can have a lot of fun," was the unwritten motto of the navvies building the line. Looking out of our sealed windows, from our air-conditioned luxury mobile pub, an iced drink in each person's hand ("Is it off the ice, mate?" you could ask a fettler of his drink. "Yairs mate. Five hundred bloody miles off the ice."), our top restaurant class meals awaiting us, the two-finger-in-the-air sign of the larrikins at their "Reconstruction Camp" cuts us down to size.

Imagination knows no limit when decorating locomotives for special trains or in celebration of special events (Victorian Railways)

THE SPECIALS

OF ALL TRAINS, be they luxury, lackadaisical, Leaping Lena's, or plodders, it's the Specials that write the punctuation marks on the railway timetables.

There have been Royal Specials, Troop Specials, Race Specials (the earliest Melbourne Cups had their own country specials), Agricultural Show trains (complete with horse and cattle boxes), Excursions, Historical Society Special trips, and Annual Picnic Specials. But the most touching of all have been the funeral trains, and perhaps the most harrowing, most anxiously awaited train of all was that bringing returning Prisoners-of-War to Perth from the seaport. For some of those waiting, it had been three years since they got the message "Missing," and no more; then with the Japanese surrender, came word of the husband, brother, or son still alive in prison camp. And so there they waited, their faces turned up the empty track, waiting for . . . .

The early picnics were fun, real swinging, laughing fun. From early dawn, the men and their wives had been up decorating the engine. "I've seen the days when the drivers' wives came down to decorate the engine for a celebration. There were dray-loads of flowers and ferns and yards and yards of bunting and flags. All of us tradesmen turned out, fitters, blacksmiths, boiler makers—everyone who could be spared—and polished the engine, the buffers shone like silver and no man would dare to shunt on them! Over the steam dome we used to put a big crown, it took two men to lift that up and lower it in place. On this crown we'd thread flowers and ferns and ribbons, all under the eyes of the women. 'No, that won't do. Take it off again!' they'd call up. 'Too much white' or 'Too many leaves,' or, 'You've crushed the bunting.' "

The Commissioners' trains which ran on country lines once a year were not decorated, but of all "Specials" they were the ones most respected by railmen ("respect" can be held to mean "to beware of"). The tales are legion about the care taken beyond the call of duty when the Commissioner's train was due, but there are just as many tales told about the things that went awry.

Gavan Duffy, a member of a long line of notable Irish legal men in Victoria (including a Chief Justice) was not a rail man, but he was such a dedicated rail fan that he was welcomed by everyone from Commissioner's down to signalmen. "How do you get in a signalbox?" he was once asked. "I've got the key. A bottle of beer." "Ever found it won't fit the lock?" "Oh yes. Sometimes I've had to use two bottles."

Once when Gavan Duffy was a supercargo on the Commissioner's train to Mildura, they were ready to leave a little platform and heard the Station Master hiss at the porter. "The ticket! The ticket!" (In the "staff and ticket" system of safe-working, a train cannot be taken out of a platform until the driver is handed a ticket.) "Give the driver the ticket!" the Station Master roared in a hiss. "Why today?" asked the lad porter, for all and sundry to hear.

Another time Gavan Duffy told this story: "I don't suppose there is any harm in relating the story of the ingenious souls who, having lost the staff between Drysdale and Queenscliff, rather than trouble their superior officers over such a trifle, fashioned a new one out of the shin bone of an ox, marked with the section names in indelible

This circus visited Australia in 1877 and gave two shows each day to 7,000 people. The circus travelled throughout Australia by special trains

Above: *450 tons of gold bound for London has been loaded on special trains at Bendigo, Victoria.*
Below: *A Tasmanian Government Railways B class locomotive has been decorated to appear as an armoured train in an effort to sell war bonds, at Waratah, Tasmania, 1918*

Above: *The Western Australian contingent bound for Transvaal awaiting the train at Karrakatta Station.*
Below: *Perth Railway Station, Western Australia, in 1945, with crowds awaiting the return by train of prisoners-of-war*

A run by the "Little Pony" and a modern diesel for the Queensland Railways Centenary in 1965

The dining car used for the visit of the Duchess of York

pencil and ran on that until the real one was found."

That the circus trains were Specials, no railway child ever forgot. "Elephants not to be loaded behind engine," read the notice to the Station Master. "An elephant once turned the tap on the engine and they ran out of water. Up near Broken Hill it was." These trains conveyed camels, horses, and mysterious crates that grunted, snorted, and squealed. Living out on the isolated country station, the kids ran up and waited when the Special was due.

"They'd stop to examine the train at a certain distance. And when they stopped at our station . . . ah, the delight, the wonder, the magic, the smell of adventure, the unknown, and far away places. Then, 'Are you railway kids?' 'Yairs.' 'Well, then, here's a couple tickets. You like the circus?' And we'd hoard those tickets, it was almost as good as going, to have real tickets." Trains did not run up to the nearest big town and back again just to take the Station Master's kids to the circus, but those tickets really were nearly as good.

The Specials that lent drama to the canvas were those called out to bring aid to beleaguered men. In the lays of the mines, as the old diggers called them, is a tale of the rescue of Varischetti who was trapped underground when working for the Westralian Gold Mine at Bonnievale, Western Australia. Varischetti, an Italian migrant who had left his four motherless children back home in Italy while he voyaged to make his fortune, was down in a "rise" south of the main shaft in No. 10 level, and did not come out when the rain began. It was Tuesday, 19 March 1907, and in four hours a downpour had filled the dry creeks, and broke the banks and the water had nowhere to go but down the mines. It rushed into the shaft of the "Westralian," and filled the main workings up to the 900 foot level. The miners clambered out only minutes before the water overtook them, but when the roll was called, Modesto Varischetti, who was working on the 1000 foot level, was missing.

The mine shaft was two-thirds full and Varischetti was down below the water level in a watery tomb. There was only one hope and that was that the onrush of water up the rise may have made sufficient compressed air to force and keep the water back. It had happened before in mining disasters. Why not now? So they set to work baling the water out and wired to Perth for diving gear. In the meantime, they picked up the faint tapping that let them know the Italian was alive—in an air pocket. The State Mining Engineer in Perth wired, "Sending diver and outfit with special train. Will wire later when expect to reach Coolgardie arrange cab meet them."

The train left Perth at 3 p.m. on 21 March with the divers and gear and was given an "open road" to Coolgardie. To save time coaling and watering, a fresh engine was hooked on at two stops on the long haul. At 4 a.m. on 22 March, the rescue train reached the goldfields, a thirteen hour journey which stood as a record for nearly fifty years until the coming of diesels.

The divers took candles and food down to Varischetti and a slate on which to write messages and, when the sun was sinking behind the scrubby mulga on 28 March, nine days and two hours since he last saw daylight, Modesto Varischetti was led out of the mine.

Diver Hughes, second from right, prepares to go down the Bonnievale mine, 22 March 1907

Construction of the standard gauge line at Windmill Hill, Western Australia, in 1968

TWILIGHT OF THE GODS

The reaction of railway enthusiasts to the death of steam was clearly described in a poem by Jack McLean, a friend of the Australian Railways Historical Society (naturally enough called by the railmen "hysterical" society). Jack writes poems mainly about "safe-working," but in this one he turns his hand to sending a get-well message to Leon, the Vicar, who was to bless the fleet of engines, but got the measles instead.

THE UNBLESSED FLEET

One Sunday at the shed, I find
A truly wonderous vision,
The Depot's locos are aligned
With military precision.
The B's and T's are spic and span
And all those lovely S's
Are shining much more brightly than
Die Lorelei's gold tresses.

The railway blokes in Sunday best
Have started an invasion
The numbers who attend suggest
A wonderful occasion.
Now why do all these rail blokes meet?
No charge made for admission?
It is the Blessing of the Fleet
A fine old rail tradition.

Just then a fireman says in jest,
" 'Twould be a damn sight quicker
In getting all these engines blessed
If we could find the Vicar."
A truth, they hear the fireman say,
It makes the meeting shiver,
The Vicar can't be here today,
He's down near Little River.

The meeting over, incomplete,
For Leon's got a sickie.
They leave the bright, but unblessed fleet
To go and have a quickie.
And as the railwaymen are plied
With alcoholic liquor,
They'll send, I hear the men decide,
Get Well Cards to the Vicar.

Above: *Loading an ore train at Jarrahdale, Western Australia.*
Below: *The famous Thursday Islander track laying team in operation on the new standard gauge line, Perth to Kalgoorlie, Western Australia*

Above: *First train on the Hamersley Iron Railway, 1968, at Dampier, Western Australia.*
Below: *The track laying machine in operation on the standard gauge line, Western Australia. It is manned by Thursday Islanders, who are also noted for their work on the Townsville to Rockhampton (Queensland) and Darwin (Northern Territory) lines*

Most railwaymen have good intent,
But draw the line at writing,
On their behalf, this card is sent,
To make your life exciting.
And so I hope that soon you may
Recover from the measles,
And come again some other day
And bless the stinking diesels.

When the second World War ended and stock was taken, the railways were in a bad way. The years of Depression had frozen stock, and manpower had been pared to a minimum; the war followed and railways were worked almost literally to a standstill. They were decrepit, worn-out, and dated—some lines were still running locomotives that had been condemned fifteen years before. Their war effort had been magnificent. The railmen and their machines had transported both Australia's and America's Pacific armies and supplies from one end of the vast continent to the other. Flying gangs on call twenty-four hours a day, seven days a week, had patched up the tracks as they threatened to collapse.

A good indication of the state of things was given in this note from Gavan Duffy, reporting in 1947. "On Friday the 14th February 1947, the Warrnambool 'Coffee Pot' driven by the 'Flying Scotchman' took twelve hours to make Camperdown from Geelong (75 miles) and had to be laid up here for the night.

"On Saturday the 15th February the Oil Burner on No. 38 Passenger threw a seven between Allansford and Cudgee. The engine of the 8.00 a.m. Special Goods came from Warrnambool and took on the train. Arrived Camperdown sixty minutes late and further delayed getting coal. This caused about thirty minutes delay to 35 Passengers. 8.00 a.m. Goods and No. 5 were both seriously delayed, the delay in the latter case being accentuated by having to wait at Boorcan while a special ex Timboon cleared.

"Then the coal burner on No. 80 Passenger Port Fairy became defective near Illowa and only just struggled into Warrnambool causing twenty-five minutes delay. After some deliberation Pomborneit and Pirron Yallock were allowed to switch out and No. 54 left Camperdown with the long section staff with just running time to Colac ahead of No. 80. Unfortunately 54 then proceeded to stall on Pomborneit Bank and had to be divided into that station and find the O.C. to unlock the signal levers causing a further delay to the Passenger of about sixty minutes. All this reacted on 73 Down Passenger which arrived here at 10.45 p.m. fifty-five minutes late."

When peace came the railway system was battered, exhausted, patched-up, and completely out-of-date. Re-organisation and planning would have to start from the bottom up.

When they paused to draw breath, they saw the whole situation and it was different. Railways had started out in competition with the bullock dray; before the war,

Facing page: *Double-banked diesels haul heavy loads of iron ore from Mount Tom Price to Dampier, Western Australia, for shipment to Japan.*
Below: *An automatic sleeper stamping machine that lifts the rails, stamps the ballast, and measures and adjusts the distance between rails*

Three diesels are needed to haul this iron ore train from Mount Newman, Western Australia

Above: *The modern method of unloading wheat, Western Australian Government Railways.*
Below: *It only takes three minutes to change bogies for differing gauges at exchange centres in Melbourne, Port Pirie, and Peterborough*

Above: *The stainless-steel Sydney to Blue Mountains (Mount Victoria) commuter train, "The Fish," Australia's oldest named train. Its counterpart on the shorter haul from Sydney to Springwood is officially titled "The Chips."*

Below: *An NSU AIA-AIA diesel-electric hauls a mixed goods train on the Darwin to Birdum line, Northern Territory*

The driver rings a bell to warn traffic as a diesel makes its way down a street in Rockhampton, Queensland

because of the depression, the motor car had not been too fearful a competitor. But what they now saw was that fast air transport and completely organised road transport had left them as far behind as they had once left the bullock wagons.

The most complete transformation imaginable must be wrought, a change as revolutionary as was the introduction of steam. It is still going on. Passenger services are being cut, and uneconomic lines closed, while machines and computers are steadily taking over. The fettlers even go to work in trucks owned by the railways— the old boys would never believe it, as they wouldn't believe the Schools for Gangers held in all States. ("My school was years on the tracks, getting my hands bitten by the dog, my shoulders bent by carrying too heavy loads, and my skin leathered by a life in the sun, wind, rain, and sand. And if I didn't learn my job that way the train fell off the line, as simple as that.")

Yet, with all the changes, the passing of steam, electrification, and streamlining, the old tradition of railway service is still one of safety and security, and a new pride in the new machines that have taken over from the old and may, in their time, become just as legendary.

The coming of "the stinking diesels" was the end of boyhood for the men who had watched the mighty iron horse thunder through ravines, conquer mountains, and blaze a trail through no-man's land. Unfortunately for their protests, steam was dead the day the cost of motive power per ton mile of diesels was estimated. (A ton-mile is the weight of freight on train multiplied by the distance travelled. This measure was introduced in 1877 by Mr Rae, an Australian Railways Commissioner and is now used internationally.) The comparative ton-mile figures of steam and diesel left no argument. In 1966 the 166 diesels of the Victorian Railways gave more ton-miles than the entire 1952 fleet of 630 steam locos had done.

It was the death knell of steam. Apart from those run as specials for historical societies, there is scarcely a steam train left in Australia. The engines that made the railways and the men who ran them appear larger than life, have become legendary. They have gone forever.

The old railmen had to learn new tricks. Tom Casey, the old Queensland driver, wrote his "New Australian Ode" about his first day on a diesel:

DRIVING THE DIESEL

When you close-a da Main Switch you getta da light
Don't let-a thiss fella give-a you da fright.

Just pressa da button pull little handle around
All-a your troubles he go to the ground.

When the air he come up to a pressure of thirty
No more show the light or the noise that so dirty

No more need now to look for da gauge
He gone away now just die of old age.

Just pressa da button each two minutes or so
No more-a da trouble as on your journey you go.

If he played up at all just turn up-a da cock
Lift up the flap you no getta da shock

You still getta da buzzer and also da light
No chance go to sleep although it be night.

No not now putta on a da brake
And from a da Engine, Power he no take.

Can't cut outa da rest just on your own
No more must-a you do before a ring on da phone.

The reference to the new engines preventing a man from having a quick sleep on duty concerns a button that the men press every two minutes. If for some reason the button isn't pressed, first a buzzer sounds, then a light flashes, and if the button is not then pressed, the train is brought to a stop by automatic brakes.

Tom was soon driving diesels as nonchalantly as he had driven steam. With other relief drivers he took the first test load over the new £5 million line from Townsville to Mount Isa.

It was by 40D on Monday
We left her for the West
With a 1300 class diesel
We thought it would be best.

To haul thirteen hundred tons
From Hughenden to Mt Isa
We felt that when the trip was o'er
That we'd be so much wiser.

And so they were. With one hundred wagons behind them, they found the faults and the advantages they had set out to find. Tom says the diesels are here to stay. They may become as legendary as steam, given time. Perhaps their wheels, singing the love song with ribbons of rails across and down and through a land as old as time, will weave a story as emotional as a folk memory. What's to say that—with the intimacy of stations on long, warm afternoons before the train departs, where lovers wait and ache with the parting, and mothers embarrass sons, the banshee wail of the express gathering speed as she reaches the open country—engines will not acquire mystery anew, the luminous self-possession of ships on broad oceans? Will this not bring a lore of its own?

The first Emu Bay Railway pyrites train near Burnie, 1970. The first train on this line was horse-drawn and carried tin from the Mount Bischoff mine

BIBLIOGRAPHY

ADELAIDE CHAMBER OF COMMERCE, *To London from Adelaide in less than Twenty-four Days* (1903) *Account of the Colony of South Australia* (1862) (anon.) BARKER, H. B. *Camels and the Outback* "BARRI COUTHA," *Railwayana* (1866) BOLAM, A. C. *Trans-Australia Wonderland* BOLTON, G. C. *Alexander Forrest, His Life and Times* *Bourke Historical Society Papers* *Bradshaw's Sydney Railway Guide* (1856) BUCHANAN, SIR G. *Report on Needs of Northern Australia re Extension of Railways* CHAMBERS, T. *The Railways of Western Australia* CLAPP, SIR H. *Report on Standardisation of Australian Railway Gauges* CORRIGAN, J. *Victorian Railways to 1962* COGHLAN, T. A. *The Wealth and Progress of N.S.W.* COMMISSIONER OF PUBLIC WORKS, S.A. *Report* (1887) DALE, G. *The Industrial History of Broken Hill* DESMOND, A. (Vet. Surg.) *Mt Serle Government Camel Depot* DOUGLAS, HON. J. *Review of Trans-continental Railway· Queensland to Darwin* (1882) EMBLING, DR A. *Address on Trans-Continental Railway* (1872) ERICKSON, J. E. *Railways and other Injuries of the Nervous System* (1866) FEARNS, R. *The Trans-Continental Railway* (1905) *Footplate*, the official organ of the Vic. and Tas. Div. of Aust. Fed. Union of Loco Enginemen FRANKLIN, LADY J. *Diary* (Archives, State Library of Tasmania) GILLMAN, B. N. *Letters, papers, etc.* (Archives, S.A.) GILDER, G. A. *Fifty years of Railway Making* GREGORY, J. W. *The Dead Heart of Australia* GUNN, MRS A. *We of the Never Never* HARRIGAN, L. J. *Victorian Railways to '62* (1962) HARDING, E. *Uniform Railway Gauge* HAY, A. *Land-Grant Railways* (1873) HARCUS, W. *History of South Australia* (1876) HELPS, A. *The Life and Labours of Mr Thomas Brassey* *Journals of the Trans-Australia Railmen—Desert Echo* (various dates) *Kelly Reward Board Report to Parliament* KENNEALLY, J. *Inner History of the Kelly Gang* LANE, R. *The Romance of Old Coolgardie* LANG, J. D. *Correspondence* (Mitchell Library) LOCO FOREMAN (Port Augusta), *Letterbook* (1879) *Mt Lyell Mining and Railway Company Records* MEDEW, R. *Unpublished MSS* MADIGAN, C. T *Crossing the Dead Heart* MUNDY, G. C. *Our Antipodes* (1852) MACKIE, F. *Diary* (Library, University of Tasmania) NEWBY, E. *The Last Grain Race* *Northern Territory Surrender Act 1907* *Northern Territory Acceptance Act 1910* *National Construction Co Ltd Records* (re tenders for construction of railway from Oodnadatta to Pine Creek) N.S.W.G.R. *The Railways of N.S.W.* (from 1885), *Rules and Regulations* (1855), *Ambulance Handbook* (1887), *Guide* (1879) *Pamphlets, Centenary of Adelaide and Port Railway, The Railway Songster* J. S. V. Turner (pub.), Launceston, *History of Launceston and Western Railway, Main Line* (Tas.) *Parliamentary Papers* (Commonwealth and State) P.W.D., Tasmania (Rly Branch), *Correspondence* PASLEY, C. *Correspondence* PRATT AND BADGER, *Railway Surveying* QUEENSLAND GOVERNMENT RAILWAYS, *A Century of Service, First Half Century* REID, A. *Those were the Days* *Report of Adelaide Meeting (1895) on Construction of Line from Oodnadatta to Darwin* (anon.) ROBBINS, M. *The Railway Age* RESIDENT ENGINEER, S.A.R. (Darwin division) *Letter Book* (1897) ROYAL COMMISSION, *Report on Trans-Continental Railway* (1887) ROYAL COMMISSION, *Report on Main Line (Tas.)* (1867-8) ROYAL GEOGRAPHICAL SOCIETY OF AUSTRALIA (S.A. BRANCH), *A Century of History of South Australia* *Silverton Tramway Company Records* SELECT COMMITTEE, *Report on Geelong-Melbourne Railway Company Bill* (1852-3) *South Australia Handbook* (1914) STONOR, CAPT. A. *A Year in Tasmania* STUART, G. *The Wheelwrights' Shop* SUTHERLAND, A. *Victoria and its Metropolis* STUCKEY, S. J. *Reminiscences* (S.A. Archives) SOUTHWELL KEELY, T. *Unofficial Report on the Northern Australia Line* THACKERAY, C. *Railway Needs* (collection of articles) THOMPSON, DEAS *Correspondence* TRENERRY, E. *Land Grant Railway* (1879) *Trans-Continental Railway Act* (1902) (Statute Book) TURNER, H. G. (pamphlet) *New South Wales Railways and Excursions to the Zig-Zag* (1869) *Van Diemen's Land Company Records* *Victorian Institute of Engineers—Proceedings* (1906) *Victorian Railways Journal* (1894-95) *Victorian Railways Telegraph Handbook* (1896) *Victorian Railways Gazette* (1891-93) VIVIENNE, M. *Travels in Western Australia* (1882) *Western Australian Historical Society Journals* *Western Australian Yearbook* (1902) WETTENHALL, R. L. *Railway Management and Politics in Victoria* (1856-1906) WHITEFORD, G. *North Australia* WHITE, W. *In Retrospect* (unpublished MSS) WILSON, A. *Lays and Tales of the Mines* YOUNG, C. D. *Railway Gates* (1853)